The Canoe: Its Selection Care And Use

Robert Eugene Pinkerton

In the interest of creating a more extensive selection of rare historical book reprints, we have chosen to reproduce this title even though it may possibly have occasional imperfections such as missing and blurred pages, missing text, poor pictures, markings, dark backgrounds and other reproduction issues beyond our control. Because this work is culturally important, we have made it available as a part of our commitment to protecting, preserving and promoting the world's literature. Thank you for your understanding.

THE CANOE
ITS SELECTION CARE AND USE

BY

ROBERT E. PINKERTON

Illustrated with Photographs

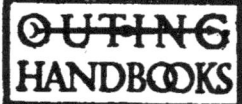

Number 48

NEW YORK
OUTING PUBLISHING COMPANY
MCMXVI

Copyright, 1914, by
OUTING PUBLISHING COMPANY

All rights reserved

An excellent type of the lake model birchcanoe. Its exceptional buoyancy is shown by the fact that the Indian weighs 225 pounds.

CONTENTS

Introduction 13

CHAPTER		PAGE
I	TYPES OF CANOES; THEIR CONSTRUCTION	17
II	CANOE MODELS; THEIR ADAPTABILITY AND USES	28
III	THE PADDLE	40
IV	PADDLING IN BOW AND STERN; THE STROKE	45
V	THE POSITION OF THE PADDLER	55
VI	PADDLING A CANOE ALONE . .	60
VII	LAKE TRAVEL	67
VIII	RIVER WORK	76
IX	PRECAUTIONS; BALLASTING THE CANOE	90
X	THE PORTAGE; METHODS OF CARRYING CANOES; THEIR CARE	97
XI	PACKING; VARIOUS METHODS; THEIR ADAPTABILITY . . .	107

CONTENTS

CHAPTER		PAGE
XII	Beds and Bedding	117
XIII	Tents for Canoeing	126
XIV	Cooking Utensils, Cooking and Foods	133
XV	Clothing	144
XVI	Making Camp: Advantages of System	155

ILLUSTRATIONS

An excellent type of the lake model birch canoe	*Frontispiece*
A canvas canoe for use on large windy lakes A good birch for rapid-filled rivers	31
Bowman beginning the draw stroke Bowman finishing the draw stroke	48
Position for throwing the canoe Indian's position in paddling	53
Best method of handling a canoe alone Canadian method of paddling	59
Yoke method of carrying a canoe	97
One or more packs may be thrown on top of the first pack	112
Canoe loaded for two weeks' trip, two persons Canoe tent, requiring two poles and seven stakes	127

THE CANOE;
ITS SELECTION, CARE AND USE

INTRODUCTION

EXPLORERS have taken canoes into nearly every quarter of the globe, even close to the North Pole, and pleasure seekers in cities have filled park lagoons with them. Thousands of men and a constantly increasing number of women plan for fifty weeks in the year on a canoe trip of two weeks, either down some civilized river or across lakes and down streams traveled only by the Indians of the north.

Across the entire continent, from Maine to Nome, Alaska, is a vast territory in which the canoe is a work horse, a carrier of burdens, as essential a part of a man's equipment as a horse on a farm.

East of the Mississippi river in the United States and east of Lake Huron in Canada are many canoe manufacturers who are turning out innumerable craft annually, supplying Hudson's Bay posts on Lake Athabasca, in Labrador, and on the MacKenzie river, the tourist in New

Brunswick, the prospector on the Yukon, the explorer of the geological survey in Ungava, the gold seeker of the Porcupine, and the bank clerk in Detriot who spends his evenings about Belle Isle with his best girl in the be-cushioned bow.

The recent growth of the use of the canoe has been as wonderful, in a way, as the little craft itself. The canoe is rapidly losing that great distrust in which the public held it. It is coming into its own, bringing with it the romance of the northland, the lure of the forest, the sane, healthy pleasure of its use.

But, despite its introduction into city parks and summer resort lakes and streams, the canoe is essentially a wilderness product, essentially a wilderness craft. And the wilderness without the canoe would be a wilderness indeed, a forbidding barrier that would shut off that vast area which is the north end of our continent as effectively as though the ice of the pole itself were interposed.

From northern Minnesota, straight north to the Arctic ocean, from the lower Ottawa to Hudson's Bay, from the St. Lawrence to Ungava Bay, and from the upper Athabasca to the mouth of the MacKenzie, the canoe has made possible the penetration of nearly every corner of the wilds, has permitted journeys which otherwise could be made only in winter or not at all.

It is in this great district that the use of the canoe, as essential to the inhabitants as the horse in the cow country, has been brought to its highest perfection, has accomplished the unbelievable. And, though vicious rips have been run, though great lakes have been crossed in heavy gales, in this lonely, northern land, it is in the city park lagoon, in the summer resort lake and river, that the craft has killed its hundreds, that it has aroused a great suspicion in the minds of many millions of people.

As ignorance and carelessness have killed their thousands with the unloaded firearm, so they have killed their hundreds with the canoe. The fact that the efficient firearm and the efficient canoe continue to prosper despite public prejudice is only an indication of their worth.

It is the purpose of this book to make the safe use of the canoe more universal, to show its possibilities, and to point out its abuses. Once the art of handling a canoe is learned, a man cannot propel a more efficient craft. Once he has learned to be its master, he has the key to a new world.

CHAPTER I

TYPES OF CANOES; THEIR CONSTRUCTION

SO far as construction and materials are concerned, canoes are made in three types— the wooden, canvas, and birchbark. The birch bark will drown the other two, but it is slower, more difficult to handle, springs leaks more easily, and becomes heavy through soaking water.

The wooden canoe is speedy, but its construction makes the finest lines impossible, and fine lines mean more than beauty. They mean seaworthiness and stability and give to a canoe that quality of being alive and intelligent, of meeting waves like conquerors and not like sawlogs.

The canvas canoe, when properly made of the best materials, is the best craft, although many experienced canoemen prefer the wooden variety so commonly used in Canada. The canvas canoe's construction is identical with that of the birch bark, after which it was patterned. It has, however, the advantage of an even, smooth surface, of greater rigidity, of faster lines. It retains its shape and is the superior of both the other types in withstanding hard usage. The well built, intelligently designed canvas canoe is really a wonderful craft. The best stock, careful workmanship, and the results of experiments and experiences have been combined until there is hardly room for improvement. The canvas covering has been rendered almost impervious to ordinary knocks and will often hold water when the planking and ribs have been crushed. If torn, it is easily mended.

The birchbark canoe, built by Indians, is, some things considered, the most wonderful craft of the three. For ten dollars I purchased a sixteen-foot canoe that rode six-foot rollers on Rainy Lake without taking a drop of water. For three dollars I once bought a twelve-foot birch that weighed little more than twenty pounds and never leaked a drop in an entire summer's travel.

But good canoe makers among the Indians are becoming scarce, forest fires have made it difficult to obtain good birch bark, and in many localities Indians are using the white man's canoes when they are able to buy them.

TYPES OF CANOES

Still, a good birchbark is to be had, though much care must be taken in selecting it. As a rule, it is better not to order it made, for the Indian will not do nearly so good a piece of work. Buy a canoe he has made for himself, and be on the ground when you buy it.

Get a canoe of three pieces. That is, a craft made with three separate pieces of birch bark on the bottom. One of two pieces, or of one, will buckle, or bulge, in the center. This greatly retards it. See that the bark is sound and not filled with many tiny holes, that it has been well sewed with the split and skinned roots of jackpine or cedar, that the thwarts and ribs are strong and the planking well placed in position. The planking will slip and expose the bark in a poor canoe.

Many birch canoes will warp and twist. Few are ever perfectly straight. Get one with the bottom, from bow to stern, as flat as possible. Indians have a habit of lifting the ends, thereby making an excellent craft for running rapids, but one almost impossible for the ordinary canoeman on windy lakes.

Treat your bark canoe with consideration, though you will be surprised to discover what hard knocks it will stand without showing a mark. Be specially careful when landing and embarking, keeping it away from rocks and snags. If possible, never get sand in the canoe. This, working down between bark and planking, gradually wears thorugh the bark, a fact which furnishes one of the greatest objections to this style of canoe.

If you have an opportunity to buy a good birch from an Indian, do not care to spend the money a white man's canoe will cost, and are willing to use it carefully, you will have a craft that will keep going when wooden or canvas canoes turn to shore. But you will travel much more slowly with the same expenditure of energy, and you must always carry a can of pitch wedged in the bow. Your craft will be harder to handle, especially in a wind, and, unless you rig some sort of a low thwart or a low seat, you must kneel in the Indian's position when you paddle.

There are several varieties of wooden canoes. In Canada this type has been in constant use for many years. In some districts any canoe, canvas or wooden, made by a white man, is called a "Peterborough," the name of the city in which wooden canoes are extensively built. A woodsman told me, in the summer of 1912, of a wonderful new canoe he had seen a few days before. His enthu-

siasm led me to expect something marvelous.
" It had a lot of wide ribs and was covered all over with painted cloth," he said.

The man, a good woodsman, had never seen or heard of a canvas canoe. In many parts of the United States the wooden canoe of the Canadians is equally unknown.

The most common form of wooden canoe is the basswood. This is made of thin boards of basswood placed over hardwood ribs six inches apart. Strips of hardwood are used to batten the cracks. Ribs and battens are generally rounded and three-quarters of an inch wide.

Another variety is known as the longitudinal strip canoe, made of strips of cedar an inch wide running from end to end and placed over hardwood ribs similar to those in a basswood craft, but closer together. Still another is the cedar rib canoe, made entirely of ribs, with only two or three longitudinal strips besides the gunwales and keel. These ribs, or arches, are one inch wide and fitted together. The last two models are wonderfully strong canoes, though the cedar is not so tough as the basswood. The cost of the rib canoe is far above that of other models, wooden or canvas.

The cedar types are light. The basswood is when it is new. Both absorb much water, the basswood becoming especially heavy on a portage at the end of a summer which calls for the expenditure of valuable energy.

One great objection to the basswood canoe now generally on the market is that it must be kept in the water. Turned over in the sun for a few hours, it opens up until it is like a sieve. Even when in use in a hot sun the upper seams will open. Dry-kiln lumber is largely responsible. The earlier product was much better. I once saw a basswood canoe that had been in use for twenty-six years.

The construction of the wooden canoe precludes the possibilities of the best lines. I have used wooden canoes that were remarkably seaworthy, but the usual model is not to be compared with a birchbark or canvas. They seem to have a stubborn rigidity that prevents a compromise with a roller.

All wooden canoes of the Canadian model are made without seats. A cross bar or thwart is placed about ten inches above the bottom. This can be used as a seat, but it is not comfortable. The intention is to have the paddlers kneel, as all paddlers should do, resting part of the weight on the thwart and part on the knees. The question of seats and kneeling is discussed in another chapter.

The canvas canoe is simply a birchbark made by a white man, with a white man's tools, with one substituted material made by white men, and with the addition of cane seats. This adherence to the Indian model permits grace and beauty in the lines, valuable, not for the artistic effect, but for the resulting efficiency.

The canoe is made over a solid mold. Ribs two to three inches wide and about a quarter or three-eighths of an inch thick are placed on the mold. The ribs are of cedar. On top are placed thin cedar planks, or strips, generally an eighth of an inch or more thick. The ribs are fastened to gunwales and hardwood stems placed at each end. Over all is stretched tightly a piece of canvas, which is filled with a preparation and given several coats of paint and varnish. The result is a craft identical, in essentials, with the Indian's canoe, only with the canvas taking the place of the birch bark.

However, that is only a simple statement of the construction. Methods, workmanship, efficiency of materials, finishing, and general knowledge of the necessities in construction vary so that canoes of all grades are produced. There are canvas canoes whose strength is almost past belief, and there are some on the market that could not stand three hundred miles in northern waters.

But the good canvas canoe, with its solid construction, keeps its shape, offers a smooth surface to the water, is light, is buoyant, will stand very hard knocks and is, all facts considered, the best all around craft.

But much depends upon the construction. The use of clear white cedar is essential. The treatment of the canvas is most important. I have seen a canoe, in the water only two weeks, show cracks and holes due to the action of the sun alone.

The compromise which must be effected between weight and rigidity is delicate, and some makers are prone to one extreme or the other. A sixty-pound canoe, carrying two 150-pound men and one hundred and fifty or two hundred pounds of duffle, is put to severe tests in riding a heavy sea or shooting a twisting, tearing current. I once saw the inwale of a canoe snapped in two when two men were riding terrific waves. There was 170 pounds in each end of the canoe, and nothing in the center. One can readily see the stress and strain that resulted in climbing and pitching over six-foot waves.

The double or open gunwale construction is best for several reasons. Manufacturers will tell you it is stronger. It has the great advantage of permitting a thorough cleaning of the canoe, something almost impossible with the closed gunwales. Sand will get into your craft, and this will work in between the planking and the canvas, as in a birchbark. In time, the threads are worn and cut, and leaks result. With open gunwales the canoe is cleaned every time it is turned over, while a little attention will keep it entirely free from sand.

And right here the canvas canoe has a great advantage over the wooden canoe, especially the basswood craft. It can be taken from the water and turned over in the sun, and, if it is a good canoe, will not be damaged. It is kept dry and light and can be carried out of the wind so that a rising sea cannot touch it.

The planking in a canvas canoe is an important feature. The edges should be matched perfectly, and the strips should run from end to end to give the best rigidity.

The construction of the ribs and the number used is most important. The greater the load a canoe is to carry, and the rougher the water to be traversed, the more rigid must be the ribbing. Some manufacturers, to meet the need for an unusually strong canoe, "double rib" the craft, placing the ribs less than half an inch apart, or build a canoe with "half ribs," which stretch only across the bottom between the full ribs. The usual spacing of the ribs in a well-made canoe is sufficient for all ordinary usage, although it is always advisable to use a floor grating. When ribs are too far apart, or planking is not continuous from bow to stern, the canoe will bend, or "hog," in the center.

The ends should be well protected by brass bang plates which should run well under the canoe. These should be riveted solidly to the stems. Manufacturers will furnish an outside stem of hardwood, which strengthens and protects, but which, like many other things, adds weight.

Some manufacturers place keels on canoes only upon request, as a rule, unless the craft be a large freight model. There is the narrow keel, about an inch deep, which strengthens the canoe and makes handling easier on windy lakes, and the shoe keel, or broad, flat protection for the bottom where rocky river beds are to be passed over. Like the outside stems, they must be considered in the compromise which one must make in the selection of his canoe, and their use or absence depends much on what is to be done with the craft.

The selection of the manufacturer depends on several things. Some sell canoes at much lower prices than others. Perhaps the best general advice is to adapt the price to the use of the canoe. If you are going to Hudson Bay, or Lake Mistisinni, or some other place far from civilization, pay the higher price. But put the money into canoe and not polished trimmings. If you are going to paddle on a small lake or city park lagoon and never leave home, the cheaper canoe will be sufficient. Don't go to the lower extreme, however. The best is none too good where a man's life depends on his canoe. The cheapest doesn't pay, even where only a sunset paddle will be the extent of your canoeing.

CHAPTER II

CANOE MODELS; THEIR ADAPTABILITY AND USES

IN this chapter the word model applies to the lines, dimensions, and shapes of canoes. There are any number of models, some manufacturers making a dozen or more, while others make only one or two. Canoes are made twelve feet long and twenty-five or thirty. They are made twenty-six inches wide and forty-six or more.

Some canoes are built solely for speed, as the Canadian racing canoe. Others are built for general use but with speed the essential consideration. Some are built for lightness, and others for strength. Most manufacturers try to reach that point where these two qualities meet. Some canoes are wide and " tubby." Others are narrow to the point of crankiness. Some are round bottomed, and others perfectly flat. Some have straight or out-flaring sides, and others have a tumble-home, or outward bulge, of one to two inches.

CANOE MODELS

Some canoes are built for racing, some for paddling in a park lagoon, some for carrying heavy loads, some for running rapids, some for climbing heavy seas in lake travel. Some canoes will weigh from a third to a half as much more than others of the same size. Some will be stiff and heavy and others so pliant they are weak and dangerous.

All these various models are built with a purpose or to try out some freak notion of a designer. I have seen canoes that seem to have been just made, purpose, thought, or possible use never seeming to have entered the head of the builder. But, as a rule, you can find a canoe built for just what you want a canoe to do. It is built for it, but it is not quite the thing, simply because perfection is impossible.

This is essentially true in out of door life. The perfect piece of equipment, tent, cooking utensil, packing contrivance, or whatever you wish, has not been made because, of necessity, everything you take into the wilderness must be a compromise. Your canoe must be a compromise, and it is only in effecting the best possible reconciliation of divergent, contradictory factors that you can approach perfection.

For instance, a canoe suited to running

rapids should have the ends raised, the bottom curved from bow to stern, that the craft may be twisted on its center, and that the current may not grip the ends. Such a canoe causes much trouble on windy lakes, for the same factor that makes it easily turned in the rapids makes it hard to keep straight in a wind.

A canoe that has good capacity and stability is slower as the greater beam and blunter bow and stern cut down the speed. A canoe that will rise with a roller, and not cut down through it, is slower than the long, tapered-bow affair. The canoe with a flat bottom is more stable and more buoyant, but it has not the speed of a round-bottomed canoe.

A canoe that is perfectly rigid, made to stand great strains and carry heavy loads, is heavy on a portage, and an extremely light canoe, for the opposite reason, will not stand the strain of a long journey in rough country. A large freight canoe will ride big seas, carry a monster load, and is strong and will stand a lot of hard usage, but it is generally too heavy for one man to carry on a portage.

Thus, your canoe must be selected for the use to which you intend to put it. Length, width, depth, construction, height of ends,

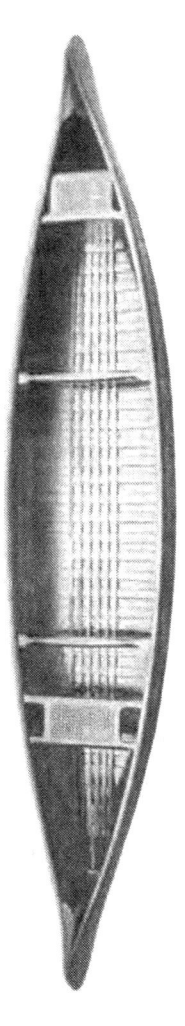

A canvas canoe built especially for use on large, windy lakes, and for carrying heavy loads. Note that the width is carried into the bow and stern not only at the gunwale but in the flat floor.

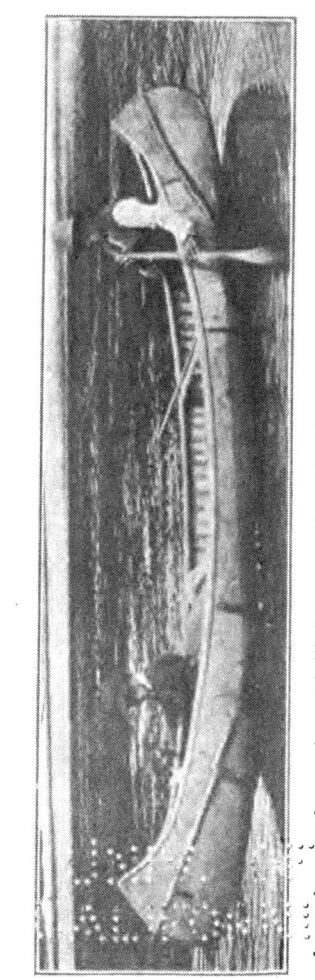

A good canoe for use in rapid-filled rivers. Note that the bottom is much lower in the centre than at the ends. The canoe is easily pivoted, and the curl of rapids will not turn it so quickly.

shape of bottom, thwarts, seats, and accessories must be considered carefully. Adapt it as nearly to the use as possible. Balance weight against strength, speed against capacity and stability, weighing the relative value of each quality.

For instance, if two men wish to take a trip down the Nepisiguit or Tobigue rivers, and intend to be in the woods two weeks, they have the following to consider: One hundred and fifty to two hundred pounds should cover food and outfit. There are many rapids. Some they will run and some they will portage around.

They should have a canoe built for river work, a slightly rounded bottom and ends raised higher than the center, on the bottom, for twisting more quickly and more safely in fast water. It should be sixteen feet long and not less than thirty-two inches wide. It should have long, slim ends for speed. The depth should be twelve inches at least. It is not necessary to have much tumble-home. The weight need not be more than sixty-five pounds. Neither can it be much less and still have the craft withstand the wrenching of the rapids and contact with rocks. A shoe keel protects the craft. This is generally half an inch thick and three inches wide in the center, tapering to the ends.

Such a canoe would not do for a trip through western Ontario, where the travel is almost entirely on lakes and where there are few rapids that can be run. If the same two men intend to spend two weeks in such a country they will have the following conditions: Many broad lakes, heavy seas, many portages of varying lengths up to two miles. These demand a flat-bottomed, straight-keeled craft thirteen inches deep and thirty-four inches wide. The ends must not be high enough to catch much wind. Wide outwales help greatly in turning combers. A good tumble home adds stability and also helps keep out the waves. The weight should be between sixty-five and seventy pounds. This will enable them to make a portage in one trip, one taking a heavy pack and the other a light pack and the canoe. The straight bottom is essential in heavy winds. The canoe will not be so apt to turn and bolt. The increased depth is necessary in heavy seas, and a canoe of that weight and size should be strong enough to stand the strain of pitching and tossing.

The width should not all be in the center, but should be carried well into the ends. The blunter bow will aid in riding waves, although it will cut down on the speed.

Consider these two men planning to float down the Ohio, the Mississippi, or some of their tributaries. The length of the trip makes little difference, for supplies may be purchased every day. There are no portages, except possibly around a dam, and then an express wagon will take all their outfit in one trip. They can take all the comforts of home, if they wish, a sheet iron stove, a large tent with dining fly, canned goods and other things with which a sporting goods house catalog is filled.

They can get a seventeen-foot canoe that weighs eighty pounds, for it will not have to be carried, and the larger canoe permits taking a larger outfit. Speed does not count for much, for the current does most of the work. There are no rapids to be run. They may, however, find some ugly seas on these rivers, especially when the wind is against a strong current. For that reason a canoe adapted to lake work, with the width carried well into the ends, a tumble- home, and a depth of thirteen or fourteen inches is best.

This is for down-stream work, however. If the canoe is to be used both up and down stream, it is better to get a faster craft with long tapering ends and keep ashore when the river gets ugly.

But we will imagine these two men are experienced canoemen, that they wish to penetrate the country west of Hudson Bay, or some district far north. They have these conditions: Large lakes, rapid-filled rivers, long, rough portages, the necessity of taking supplies for two or three months.

They want a canoe that will ride seas, and such a canoe can, if necessary, run rapids. So they take the straight-keeled craft and depend upon their skill to handle it in fast water. They will take a sixteen-foot canoe thirteen or fourteen inches deep, thirty or thirty-six inches wide, and of about seventy pounds weight. They will select a good make and pay a good price, for a canoe of that weight must be wonderfully well made to stand the strain to which they will put it. A saving in purchase may cost dear in the end.

They will have a canoe with a good tumble-home and one in which the width and flat floor are carried well into the bow and stern, for both these features increase the carrying capacity and buoyancy and add to the seaworthiness.

With such a craft they can carry three or

four hundred pounds of equipment and food and be able to make good time and live out a good gale. They will not have too much canoe to carry on portages and every pound counts when you are to be gone two or three months. Their craft should withstand rough usage and come back sound as when it started, except for a possible patch or two on the canvas. The necessary supplies for making repairs are mentioned elsewhere.

But if these two men decide to stay at home and paddle about the park lagoon, they do not have to consider capacity, width, weight, rigidity, high ends, and what-not. They want a craft that paddles without much effort, that has quite a bit of speed. They want a canoe that is graceful, with the high ends Indians are supposed to build, and that has a bright coat and shining gunwales and decks. They get a sixteen-foot canoe thirty-one or thirty-two inches wide, with a bottom somewhat rounded and with long, tapering ends. All these factors go for speed and ease in paddling. It will be eleven inches deep, which brings down the weight, adds to the beauty and grace, and is sufficient for the waves they will encounter. It need not have great carrying capacity, for they will never carry more than a basket of lunch. And their canoe, unsuitable for a trip in the wilderness, is as smart a looking craft, and as sufficient for their purpose, as any made.

The following are the essential factors to be remembered in selecting a canoe, it being assumed that the length is sixteen feet:

In quiet waters the depth need be no more than eleven inches. For rivers it should be twelve inches, for lake travel thirteen, and on a long journey, where the load is to be heavy, it should be fourteen.

The width may be thirty-one inches for quiet water and where speed is desired rather than capacity or stability. As greater capacity and stability are required, the width should be increased to thirty-five or thirty-six inches in the center and bow and stern broadened at the bottom and on the gunwales.

For river work the canoe should have the ends raised, the bottom bowing upward from the center, but for lake work the keel should be straight. For heavy lake work a good tumble-home is best, and to get a maximum of seaworthiness and capacity the width should run well into the ends. A rounder bottom gives speed at the sacrifice of stability. A flat bottom gives capacity and stability at the expense of speed, unless the canoe be heavily loaded. Then the flat-bottomed craft is faster.

Have open gunwales that the life of the canvas be prolonged, unless your canoe is to be used at a summer resort for pleasure only, and you use a carpet, pillows, tennis shoes, etc. Then the closed gunwale construction is much neater.

When a canoeman desires to decrease or increase the length of his craft the same general factors should be considered. One man and his pack can travel almost anywhere in a thirteen-foot canoe that should weigh fifty pounds. The depth, for rough travel, should be thirteen inches and the width at least thirty-four. A flat bottom with a good tumble-home will give better stability and capacity, necessary in so short a craft. Such a canoe can carry two men, though the length prohibits dryness in rough water.

The same general factors cover the fourteen and fifteen-foot canoes. A fifteen-foot canoe is suitable for two persons in rough lake travel if the load is not too heavy and if the beam is at least thirty-five inches and the depth thirteen inches.

If three persons intend to use one canoe,

the length should be eighteen feet, though I have made a two weeks' journey on rough lakes with two other persons, complete equipment, and food in a fifteen-foot river model canoe. But it is not advisable. Too much care and exertion in heavy winds are required, the heavy load makes rapid travel too strenuous, and the craft's buoyancy is reduced to such an extent that waves easily come over the bow.

A seventeen-foot canoe, for three persons and equipment, should be thirty-six or thirty-seven inches wide and fourteen inches deep. Every foot you add puts five pounds into a canoe, and, by carrying the width toward the ends, you can get the same capacity in a sixteen-foot canoe as in a seventeen, and so on up. The greater length, on the other hand, gives more room for paddlers and duffle. Such a craft eighteen feet long should be thirty-five inches wide or more and at least thirteen inches deep.

Past the eighteen-foot class one enters the realm of the freight canoe, which may be most anything you wish. For instance, a twenty-foot canoe forty-three or forty-four inches wide and nineteen inches deep will weigh nearly two hundred pounds, but will have a capacity of about 2,500 pounds. The selection of such a canoe should depend upon the amount of freight, the nature of the going, and the efficiency of the canoemen.

Where there are four in a party, however, it is better to use two canoes of sixteen-foot length and suitable to the journey—rivers, lakes, length of trip, etc. Then, if anything happens to one party, there is still a canoe. There is an extra canoe to portage, but a canoe large enough for four would require two men in the portaging, so nothing is lost there. Better time may be made, and each of the four men may paddle more effectively.

It has not been the intention in this chapter to convey the idea that a canoe fit for rivers is unsuitable entirely, or even dangerous, for lakes, and *vice versa*. The object has been to point out the qualities which are essential for an efficient craft in each department of work.

CHAPTER III

THE PADDLE

THE proper paddle is essential for accurate, easy, and strong propulsion of a canoe. Though a most important feature in canoeing, comparatively little consideration is given to the selection of a paddle, even by experienced canoemen.

Paddles are made of spruce, cedar, maple, ash, and pine. The paddle most generally furnished by canoe manufacturers is made of spruce or maple. Cedar, ash, and pine paddles are generally those made by Indians for their own use.

The canoeing paddle is a single-bladed affair, although the double-bladed arrangement, usually eight and one-half to ten feet long, is sometimes used. The most efficient work is done with the single-bladed paddle, and its use is practically universal.

The first consideration in the selection of a paddle is the length. The accepted rule is that the paddle should be as long as the user

THE PADDLE

is tall. This is true if paddling is done from a seat. In paddling from the knees, the paddle may be three inches shorter, though the full length is better. The rule does not apply to bow paddlers. In that position, especially if paddling is done from the knees, the implement should be three inches shorter than the height of the paddler. A bow paddler can work with a paddle a foot shorter than he is tall, but the stern man has difficulty if the paddle is six inches shorter than his height.

Two woods, spruce and maple, are chiefly used. Paddles made of spruce are thick, strong, and light. They are also very unyielding. Paddles of maple are heavy, strong, and with a certain amount of spring. The spruce paddle wears and frays quickly if used in rapids, for breaking ice in the fall, or if used for poling in shallow water. The ragged edge must be trimmed often, an operation which continually reduces the size of the blade. The spruce paddle, also because of its thickness and softness, does not enter or leave the water silently or freely.

The best paddle for all-round use is that made of maple. There is a tendency on the part of manufacturers, however, to produce a paddle too thick and heavy. Such paddles have all the deficiencies of the spruce paddle, excepting wear, without the advantage of being light, and they do not have sufficient spring.

The maple paddle will stand much more abuse, especially when used as a pole or in rapids, and the strength of the wood permits a thin blade that enters and leaves the water cleanly. Because of the heaviness of the material, the maple paddle should be made from the finest straight-grained wood, that the lightest, thinnest implement consistent with strength may be possible. The usual paddle does not come up to such a standard.

For long cruises in the wilderness the maple paddle is the superior. The spruce paddle, in fact, because of its stiffness, is entitled to a place only in a racing canoe.

The experienced canoeist always tests the "spring" of a paddle the moment he picks it up. For racing, the stiff, unyielding blade is desirable, but for the grind of an all-day journey, a paddle that "gives" softens the shock of quick, hard strokes. The advantage of a "springy" paddle is also felt in the recovery. If the paddle is given a final snap at the end of a stroke, the spring of the blade will shoot it forward for the next stroke with little effort on the part of the paddler.

Paddles are made with blades of several shapes, the design varying with the district. The size of the blade is of more importance. Too large a blade makes the work too heavy; too small a blade results in wasted energy. A large blade is held almost stationary in the water, and the shock and strain on arms and shoulders are too severe. For the opposite reason, a small blade does not remain stationary in the water and does not afford a sufficient purchase for efficient propulsion or handling.

The size of the blade, of course, must depend upon the size and strength of the paddler. For the usual canoeist a blade five and one-half inches wide and two feet eight or ten inches long is sufficient.

Manufactured paddles invariably are made with a knob or grip at the end of the shaft for the upper hand. Many Indians make paddles with straight, tapering shafts. While their mode of paddling makes the straight shaft preferable, there is still a question as to the grip being essential to a white man. In any event, he can often ease strained muscles by grasping the shaft below the grip, the thumb side of the hand being nearer the blade and the back of the hand toward the paddler.

Paddles made by canoe manufacturers invariably are varnished. While this adds to the life of the paddle, it is hard on the hands. If one has a varnished paddle it is better to scrape the varnish from the shaft at the points where it is grasped. The natural wood will not blister so badly. An oiled paddle absorbs water after a time and becomes heavier. This can be avoided if the application of oil is renewed occasionally.

Any paddle, varnished or oiled, should not be left in the sun, especially after it has been long in the water. It will check, or split. Paddles should be watched and the tips trimmed when they become ragged.

An emergency paddle should always be carried. On a long trip it is essential and should be placed always within easy reach of the stern paddler. Then, in case of accident, either in rips or a heavy sea, he need not miss a stroke. Even on a sunset paddle, an emergency blade will come in handy should the one in use be dropped or broken.

CHAPTER IV

PADDLING IN BOW AND STERN; THE STROKE

PADDLING a canoe is like any other wilderness activity. It is a matter of practice and experience, of instinctive and unconscious movement. It is as difficult to teach as horseback riding or skating.

Primarily, it is the action of thrusting a paddle forward, catching the water and pulling the canoe up to and past it. Two beginners in a canoe at once paddle on opposite sides because they find they work against each other. They are satisfied with this fact and continue to waste energy, each forcing the canoe ahead, but also diagonally across the course toward which the other's efforts tend. The paddler in the stern finds that he more than overcomes the turning tendency of the other and loses still more time and strength trailing his paddle to hold the canoe straight.

Gradually both bowman and stern paddler acquire the belief that the stern man must do all the steering, that he may take time from forcing the canoe forward to do so, and that the bowman must only paddle always with the same stroke and with as much energy as his temperament or inclination decrees.

Both become accustomed to the rising and falling of the canoe in small waves. As they venture into large waves each unconsciously balances the craft as it passes over a crest. They still paddle as when they began, although accustomed muscles and practice have made their strokes more regular and stronger.

And these two paddlers will go through their canoeing days with no greater knowledge unless much experience in rough waters teaches the necessity of many tricks with the paddle and brings those instinctive, unconscious movements which mark the experienced canoeman.

To begin with the bowman. The first and general belief that his only duty is to sit in front and paddle should be dispelled. First, he must set a steady, regular stroke that never varies in inclination of the paddle or in the strength applied. His stroke must be machine like. He should not throw his paddle forward and sweep it back in the most natural way. This swings the bow in the opposite direction.

THE STROKE

Practice, study, and experience will teach him that, by starting his paddle farther away from the bow and bringing it back in a nearly straight line to his side, he will devote practically all the energy expended to forcing the canoe straight ahead. He will see that his former stroke, starting closer to the bow and sweeping back in an outward arc, has always forced the bow in the opposite direction. This, in addition to his own diverted energy, calls for wasted effort on the part of the stern paddler in swinging the canoe back or in holding it against the oblique course.

The foregoing applies to straight paddling on a lake without a heavy sea. Near shore, where there are rocks, snags, or logs, either above or below the surface, in rivers where swift currents twist, or in small streams where sharp bends are to be made, the bowman becomes equally responsible with the stern man in steering. Many times he must assume all the responsibility. It is then that the bowman, to be a good bowman, must have the ability to "draw" and to "throw" a canoe. All this can be done from the side on which he is paddling and generally without a cessation of his forward propelling efforts. Few bowmen realize the possibilities of their position, however. Even the man considered skilled at the summer resort or park knows little or nothing of what a bowman should do. It is in the wilderness, where constant paddling and meeting all sorts of conditions are the rule, that the efficient bowman is developed.

Let the bowman first understand that he is as important to the speed and safe passage of the canoe as the stern paddler. Let him understand that his strength and skill are as essential in turning or keeping the course as the other's. Let him understand that his is the sole duty of setting a regular, efficent stroke, that his is the chief duty of watching for rocks and snags beneath the surface, that his is the duty of passing back information as to the course which the stern paddler cannot obtain because of his position. In short, let him understand that he must be more than a machine or working passenger.

Once the bowman has learned the most effective way of propelling the canoe straight ahead, without obliquely tending efforts, he can take up the subject of his own duties and possibilities in steering. To " draw " the canoe, he merely reaches far out to the side and pulls. By pulling toward himself at an angle of forty-five degrees to the canoe he not only turns the

Bowman beginning the draw stroke.

Bowman finishing the draw stroke. Note by the wake how quickly the canoe has been turned with only slight loss of momentum.

canoe in the desired direction, but he also maintains the forward motion. The angle at which he pulls must be adapted to the quickness of the turn to be made. If an unusually sharp bend is to be negotiated, or the canoe turned about quickly, the propelling force should come entirely from the stern while the bowman pulls the bow around. This is the opposite of the generally conceived idea, but it is the most effective. The bowman, to do this, can reach out at right angles and pull straight toward himself, or he can, more effectively, hold his paddle in the water, turn the forward edge of the blade outward and lean heavily upon the shaft. If the canoe has little or no momentum, he may pull the bow around quickly by keeping his paddle in the water, leaning heavily upon it and working it forward and back, slightly turning the blade so that the leading edge is always away from the canoe.

Proficiency in these strokes is not easy to acquire, but practice, study, and experience will soon open a bowman's eyes to the possibilities of his position in the canoe and enable him and his companion to turn sudden river bends without that disheartening loss of momentum.

All this has applied, however, only to turning the canoe toward the side on which the bowman is paddling. To turn in the opposite direction, the bowman must change sides or be proficient in "throwing" the canoe, the most difficult thing he has to learn. In many instances there is not time to change the paddle from one side of the canoe to the other when a sub-surface rock shows dead ahead, and even in a twisting stream it is bothersome. But to throw a canoe requires much practice and a strong wrist. Except for my own "bowman," I have known only one paddler who could do it efficiently, although there are undoubtedly many others.

"Throwing" the canoe is based on the principle above mentioned that there is less loss of momentum in making short turns if the stern paddler furnishes the motive power. The bowman becomes the steersman. His paddle is held perpendicularly, the blade in the water and its forward edge straight ahead. The lower hand must hold the paddle rigidly, while the upper hand turns the blade as though it were a rudder. This should be done slowly and cautiously. A quick turn permits the water to wrench the paddle around so that the flat blade stops the canoe. To turn it even slightly results in a wrench that tests the lower wrist and the grip of the upper hand. But, if the paddle, which really becomes a rudder, is held firmly, the bow is lifted and quickly shot over to the opposite side and the rock evaded or the turn negotiated, the stern paddler, during the operation, having continued to force the canoe forward, helping to turn, of course, as he can.

This position of the paddle is a good one to maintain when approaching a shore. By a quick twist either way, the bowman can direct the canoe to a safe landing with the utmost delicacy. Caution is necessary, however, in "throwing" a canoe. If the momentum be great, the paddle may be wrenched under the canoe and the craft capsized.

Before the bowman has acquired this knowledge and perfected himself in these strokes, the stern paddler has become proficient. In efficient paddling the stern man has much less to learn, although, in the usual canoeing party, he is the most skilled. But, if he has a less number of strokes and tricks in which to perfect himself, he still has many other things to study. The first will be the usual straight-ahead stroke. At first he trails his paddle, using it as a rudder at the end of each stroke, to keep the canoe straight. Even with an efficient bowman, his own misdirected efforts tend to a constant deviation from the course. Gradually he learns that, by ending his stroke with a slightly outward shove, and by twisting his paddle so that the inner edge of the blade leads the other, he accomplishes the same result without the loss of time or wasted effort.

In time, the slight variations of this stroke necessary to conditions that change constantly, as on a windy lake, become instinctive and automatic, and he may paddle in a straight line without close attention to the task.

As the bowman must assume much of the steering responsibility in a twisting river, the stern paddler assumes it all in open water travel. With a bowman propelling a canoe as he should, the stern man reaches the stage where he performs his task unconsciously.

The usual stroke of the amateur canoeist is a long, slow pull with a slow, sweeping recovery. In the north woods, where the canoe is best understood, this stroke is never seen. The stroke is shorter, the recovery like lightning, and nearly two strokes are taken to the amateur's one.

A day's journey will demonstrate the superiority of the woodsman's methods. His quick

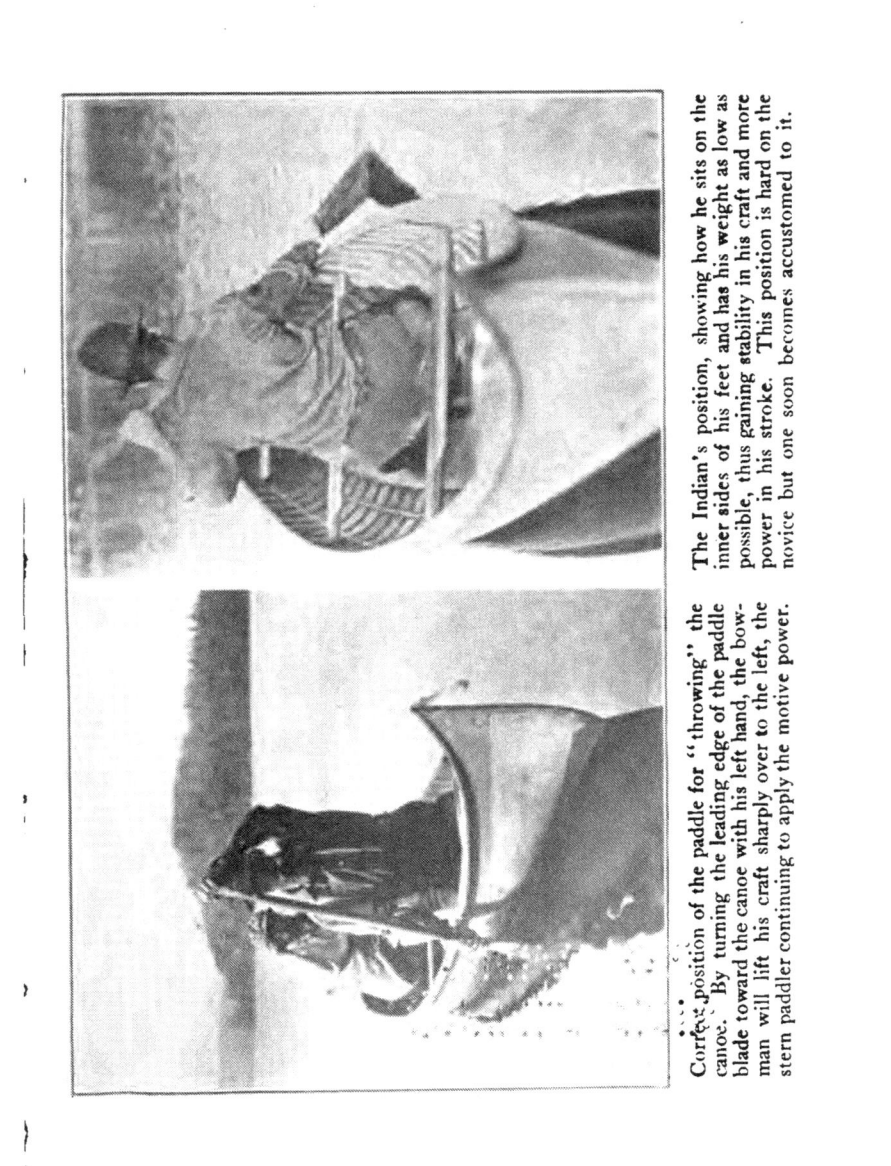

Correct position of the paddle for "throwing" the canoe. By turning the leading edge of the paddle blade toward the canoe with his left hand, the bowman will lift his craft sharply over to the left, the stern paddler continuing to apply the motive power.

The Indian's position, showing how he sits on the inner sides of his feet and has his weight as low as possible, thus gaining stability in his craft and more power in his stroke. This position is hard on the novice but one soon becomes accustomed to it.

THE STROKE

recovery almost eliminates that loss of momentum which is so hard to overcome and which is a continual drag on the energy of the slow-stroked paddler. The canoe maintains its headway, and greater results are accomplished for the energy expended.

The woodsman devotes his strength to the first of the stroke. The power diminishes rapidly when the paddle reaches his side, and the stroke is terminated quickly after it has passed. To continue the stroke as far back as one can reach necessitates a sharp inclination of the paddle. Any force expended upon the paddle when it is so inclined serves to pull the paddle up through the water more than to push it backward. The result on the canoe is to force or pull down the stern rather than to add to the forward motion. Not only is energy diverted from propulsion, but the upward lift on the paddle forces the stern more deeply into the water, thereby causing a greater drag on the canoe.

The quick, short stroke has another advantage which saves time and energy. With the proper paddle, the spring of the blade itself is sufficient to shoot the paddle forward for the next stroke with but little effort on the part of the paddler. To do this, the lower hand should be rigid at the end of the stroke, and there should be a slight, quick addition of power just before the paddle leaves the water.

The university oarsman, with his long sweep and sliding seat, takes from thirty to forty-two strokes to the minute. The usual racing stroke is about thirty-six. Loss of momentum is one of the things most carefully guarded against. The canoeist, even though he be plodding along hour after hour instead of racing, can benefit by the same principle. It is for this reason that the woodsman takes nearly twice as many strokes as the park lagoon paddler.

The usual slow paddler takes twenty-five to twenty-eight strokes to the minute. The woodsman, with his quick recovery and shorter stroke, takes forty-four to forty-seven. He travels faster with less expenditure of energy. In repeated trials I have found that the quick, short stroke is far less tiring in addition to accomplishing greater results.

CHAPTER V

THE POSITION OF THE PADDLER

BEFORE going farther with the subject of paddling, the question of seats, or their absence, should be considered. The cane seat, built in practically all canoes made in the United States, is strictly a white man's addition to the craft. Undoubtedly it was called for by the infrequent use of the canoe and consequent inability or dislike of the canoeist to assume the position of the original paddler, the American Indian. To-day the use of the cane seat is so common in the United States that few realize the existence of another method.

The first canoeman, the Indian, did not put a seat in his canoe because he knew it lessened his paddling power and decreased the stability of his craft. The Canadian, who has used the canoe far more than residents of the United States, did not place a seat in his canoe, nor did he adhere to the Indian method of sitting on the inner sides of his feet. He effected a compromise by placing a broad thwart about ten inches above the bottom and kneeling, with his hips resting on the thwart.

For the most effective paddling, for insured steadiness of the canoe, for better control over the craft, and for greater safety in rough water, either lake storms or rapids, the kneeling position is the best.

The reasons are obvious, if the subject is given close study. Stability becomes greater the lower the load in the canoe and the less the weight on the gunwales. To abandon the seat, which is fastened on the bottom, manifestly tends to increase stability. To assume the Indian's position, which brings the hips to within two or three inches of the bottom, affords even greater stability, for all the load is on the bottom, the weight is as low as possible, and the swinging lever of the body is so greatly shortened that any swaying motion has less effect.

For all except ordinary conditions, the Canadian's position is sufficient, so far as stability is concerned. In extremely nasty going it may be necessary for the paddler to abandon his thwart and get lower, in the Indian's position. Such necessity is very rare, however.

For travel in quiet waters or on calm lakes, it may be argued that the cane seat is permissible. It is, so far as stability is concerned, but it does not permit the most effective propulsion of the canoe. The university oarsman uses his legs and body far more than his arms in driving the shell. The man who rows from a stationary seat does not depend entirely upon his arms, but has his legs braced and uses their strength and that of his back. But the paddler, sitting erect on a seat, cannot use any muscles except those of his arms and shoulders. He exerts a strain on those of his back and hips, but that strain is necessary to retain a firm contact with the canoe and does not serve to aid propulsion.

The knee paddler, by falling forward onto his paddle at the beginning of his stroke, is permitted to use his back and thigh muscles in propulsion, and practically all exertion is directly applied to driving his craft. He either can attain a greater speed for the same expenditure of energy as the seat paddler, or he can maintain the same speed with less exertion.

There are two additional advantages in knee paddling. The man on a seat sits on his canoe, clings to it. The knee paddler wedges his knees against the side, braces against the thwart and becomes a part of his craft, just as the cowpuncher becomes a part of his horse. He has his canoe under better control in balancing, propelling, and handling. Further, in a breeze, he offers less of his body to the wind and can more easily forge ahead. This last is an important factor in an all-day struggle against a head wind.

There is only one real objection to paddling from the knees, and that is the consequent discomfort to the beginner. He cannot remain in that position long at a time. But it comes with practice and can be worked into gradually. The man physically fit and hardened soon grows accustomed to the position. The city man who spends his evenings on a lake or a few weeks at a summer resort or in the wilderness will have a more difficult time of it. But it is worth enduring a little pain to acquire the knack of knee paddling. The compensation is more than will be expected, and some day, on a gale-swept stretch of water, it may mean the paddler's life or that of a companion.

The best way to learn is to start the first day of a trip. When impeded circulation and cramps make it painful, get back into the seat, or sit on the thwart if there are no seats. Rest

The best method of handling a canoe alone, whether the craft be light or loaded. More power may be applied, and a light canoe will run better, if the craft is tipped far to one side.

The Canadian method of paddling, a compromise between the Indian's position and the American's cane seat. The paddlers kneel on the bottom, resting the hips on the broad thwarts set below the gunwales.

a short time, and then try the knees again. In a few days you will be doing all your paddling from the knees and be glad that you are able to do so.

Manufacturers of the best canoes will build canvas craft with the Canadian's thwart instead of the cane seat without extra charge.

CHAPTER VI

PADDLING A CANOE ALONE

TWO men in a canoe learn to paddle with certain strokes. When there are three or four there is practically no difference. There are few, except where men are accustomed to traveling much alone, who can, single handed, properly handle a canoe under all sorts of conditions.

The common method of handling a canoe alone is to turn the craft around, using the bow for the stern, and sit on the bow seat or kneel before the bow thwart, if there are no seats. The object is to bring the paddler's weight nearer the center of the canoe and keep more of the craft in the water that stability may be increased. With a load, the lone canoeman generally places it far forward and uses the stern seat, or thwart, in the usual way because he finds he has difficulty in handling the canoe except when close to the rear end. Many place a weight in the bow to hold it down and paddle from the stern seat.

Under favorable conditions—running down stream in good water, on a calm lake or with a breeze straight behind—such methods result in easy handling. Running rapids singly, on windy lakes with the wind ahead or on the beam or quarter, or crossing whirling, twisting currents or whirlpools, such a position in a canoe is impossible for adequate handling. A man may make some progress, but the energy expended is altogether out of proportion to that necessary, while in an extremely heavy wind any progress is impossible.

The correct manner in which to paddle a canoe alone, either with or without a load, is from the center. This is the method employed by the Indians, and it has been adopted by the most efficient white canoemen, those who live in the north country.

With the canoeman in the center, or a few inches aft, the canoe rides on practically an even keel. It draws less water and travels faster. There is no drag at the stern as is the case when the bow is riding high out of the water. Greater speed is possible.

But the great advantage of paddling from the center lies in the greater control the canoeman has over his craft. Sitting in the stern, or even using the bow seat and turning the canoe around, the paddler is still far from the forward end. A wind or current may grasp the bow and whirl him about readily. The long stretch of canoe without a paddle acts as a large lever, and in a bad wind human strength and skill are powerless to keep the craft headed in the direction desired. If the lone paddler sits in the stern of a light canoe, he not only is powerless in a wind, but the greatly decreased stability of the craft, and the large amount of the canoe out of the water and offered to the wind, make his position dangerous. When he paddles from the bow seat he does not eliminate the trouble, but only diminishes it.

Paddling from the center, the canoeman has his craft under as nearly perfect control as is possible. Wind or currents have an equal effect on bow and stern, or nearly so, and, because of his position, the paddler can pull, push or hold either bow or stern more nearly where he wants them. In such a position he can hold his canoe straight into a bad wind, while he also may quarter into it or quarter away from it. In fact, it is the only position in a canoe which permits travel in a gale.

There is an added advantage in the middle position in that it affords a light bow and stern which, in turn, mean a dry canoe even in a heavy sea. The canoe rises and falls instantly with each wave and is not so stiff that it antagonizes a comber and takes splash or spray over the gunwales. The man who paddles alone from the stern, with his load far forward, lacks this advantage and takes water, which is both uncomfortable and dangerous.

In carrying a load in a canoe, paddling from the stern is as easy and equally advantageous if running before a light or even stiff wind, or if paddling on calm waters. With a stiff breeze in any other direction, however, the load should be placed both before and behind the paddler in such a manner as to permit a practically even keel. In order to gain the advantage of a light bow and stern for heavy seas, the load should be placed as near the paddler as possible.

Paddling from the center is a trick in itself for the canoeman, and, no matter what his skill in bow or stern with another paddler, he will have difficulty in mastering the center stroke. A little experimenting, a study of cause and effect, and he will be better fitted to begin practicing. Once the stroke is acquired, it becomes as automatic and unconscious as that in bow or stern.

The best position for the center stroke is to kneel. In nearly all Canadian canoes the center thwart is placed ten or twelve inches aft of the center. The lone canoeman kneels in front of this thwart, resting his hips upon it. His weight is then a few inches aft of the center. The kneeling position brings the canoeist lower, and he must be nearer the water than when paddling in bow or stern.

The first stroke the beginner will take in such a position, and the most natural stroke, will be to start the blade near the canoe and sweep it back and away from him in an arc, the stroke ending, as it began, with the paddle against the canoe. Instantly the canoe will turn. Four such strokes will turn it completely around. So the beginner starts his stroke in the same manner, carries it through in the same way, and ends it by trailing his paddle and pulling the canoe back into and past the line of travel. This results in a course similar to that of a snake in motion, with the canoe turning first far to one side and then far to the other side of the line of travel. That means a great waste of energy and loss of momentum.

To paddle correctly from the center, and to keep the canoe traveling in a straight line, it is necessary to start the stroke, not close to the canoe, as would be natural, but out from it. Half way through, the stroke is close to the gunwale and moving straight back. Immediately after it has passed the paddler, it is turned outward, finishing slightly away from the canoe. The result is that the bow, at the beginning of the stroke, instead of being turned away from the paddle, is held straight, and the stern, at the end of the stroke, instead of being pulled toward the paddle, is kept in line.

The last of this stroke is uncomfortable and tiring. The most efficient and easy stroke starts away from the canoe, moves straight toward the gunwale at the paddler's side and then continues straight back along the canoe. However, as the paddle passes the canoeman, the blade is turned so that the inner edge leads the outer edge. The inclination of the paddle increases, until, as the paddle is taken from the water at the end of the stroke, the blade is at an angle of forty-five degrees to the canoe.

Such a stroke results in the canoe traveling straight ahead with little or no deviation from the course if there is no wind. In a heavy sea, of course, it is varied to meet conditions.

Much practice is necessary to attain perfection in paddling from the center, and few canoemen will take the trouble to learn it unless compelled to do much traveling alone on windy lakes. Once the stroke has been perfected, however, the paddler will prefer it to any other.

It is advisable for the beginner to kneel directly over the keel until he has begun to master his stroke. Once he is part of his canoe, he can begin to move out toward the gunwale. When he is a skilled center paddler his side will be against the gunwale, and his canoe will be tipping at a seemingly dangerous angle. However, it will run better on its side, and the position nearer the gunwale permits more power being put into the stroke and better control over the canoe.

The side position is best under nearly all circumstances. The paddlers, where two are in a canoe, can balance each other if they move out toward the gunwales. The paddle held perpendicularly is always more efficient than that which crosses the breast of the canoeman.

CHAPTER VII

LAKE TRAVEL

THE two conditions of canoe travel demanding great skill are those of open water and white water. In either only experience will bring proficiency. Instruction is inadequate and difficult. Set rules cannot fit conditions which are never twice alike. Each wave on a large lake has as much individuality as the usual stretch of rapids. Not only knowledge, but a well developed ability to act instinctively, automatically, and unconsciously is necessary. This comes only through experience. There can be only, on such a subject, a number of general cautions and rules, all of a certain elasticity and adaptability.

In lake travel the canoeist probably meets the greatest test. Rapids may be dangerous, but they decide quickly. There is a moment of tensity and an exhilaration, mingled with a feeling of utter helplessness, and you are safely through or are struggling in the water. On a broad lake, white-capped and squall-swept, the fight may go on for hours. There is no opportunity to rest, to relax tense nerves and muscles, to ease the strain.

The ability of a good canoe to live through a gale is little less than marvelous. Provided it is of the proper model, well handled, and properly loaded, a canoe will live through most anything. The greatest difficulty comes in reaching the desired destination.

One common misconception of the canoe is that it cannot take a sea broadside, cannot travel in the trough. But, for a skilled canoeist, there is no safer or easier direction in which to take the wind. The canoe handles more easily, better time can be made, and less water will be taken. The only requisite is an ability to balance instinctively, and this comes only with practice and experience.

In traveling across the wind the canoe merely rises and falls with the waves. It is only when the crest is reached, and the craft starts down the windward side, that a supreme nicety in balance is necessary, that there is danger of taking water or even of capsizing. If the waves are breaking badly, as in a quick squall, it is necessary to head the canoe slightly into the wind, so that the force of the breaking comber is taken farther forward.

In this connection it is best to fix the status of the bowman in any sort of bad water. Under no circumstances should he ever try to balance the canoe by leaning to one side or the other, or by holding his paddle in the water. From his position he is unable to see how a wave is affecting the canoe. The stern paddler has the entire situation before him. He alone is in a position to maintain the proper balance, and he alone should do it. No matter how far the canoe leans one way or the other, the bowman should maintain his position and keep paddling. This applies to rapids as well as to taking seas at any angle, both delicate operations.

The best instance of the necessity of such lack of action on the bowman's part is had in heading slightly into the wind when taking heavy seas on the beam. The bow, slightly to the windward of the stern, climbs the sea to the crest with a quick, bouncing motion. It shoots out over the crest, is suspended in mid air for an instant, and then jerks down. At the same time the stern bounces up. Simultaneously, there is a quick shifting of the support of the canoe by the water and a consequent, instantaneous tilt from leeward to windward. The stern paddler alone can see the exact moment when his weight must be shifted sufficiently to prevent taking water. Should the bowman also act, the stern paddler's delicate poise would be disturbed, and water would be shipped or the canoe capsized.

On a large lake, where there are long rollers, riding waves in the trough is comparatively easy and lacking in danger. If the seas are short and choppy, water will splash in. On a large river, like the Mississippi, where a heavy wind against a strong current piles up high, short, combing waves, there is always danger, traveling in any direction, and only a skilled paddler should attempt such a sea. Riding the trough becomes especially dangerous here because of the opposite forces of gripping current and wind.

Quartering away from the wind is comparatively easy and safe. Quartering into it is harder and requires great delicacy, not only in balancing as the canoe takes an oblique plunge over the roller, but the craft must be nursed carefully that a stiff bow is not offered to a comber. Ability to handle waves on the bow comes comparatively quickly. It is largely a question of forging ahead between waves and easing up on the power as the boat meets the crest.

In taking the wind on the quarter, either fore or aft, it is impossible to keep the point from slueing around several points on each wave. The stern paddler needs only to retard this tendency. To prevent it entirely means a waste of strength and to hold the craft solidly against a wave, with a consequent taking of water over the gunwales.

Running before the wind is much like taking it on the quarter. Practically all the stern man's strength is needed to keep the canoe straight, for slue around it will when a roller passes beneath it. A perfect balance only is necessary to keep the craft dry, provided it is not loaded too heavily.

Bucking straight into a gale requires eternal watchfulness, endurance and patience. A pugnacious spirit may prove disastrous. Every wave cannot be conquered. With most a compromise must be effected.

Many canoeists make the mistake of traveling too fast against a heavy wind. This results in the bow plunging into a wave and taking water. To drive a canoe hard against the wind also results in the bow shooting out over the crest and dropping with a thud onto the next wave. This not only causes the spray to fly and the canoe to stop, but it is hard on the craft. A paddle blade may be split by striking it flat against the water. What must be the result when a canoe drops with a bang, the bottom striking flatly against the side of a wave?

In a short, choppy sea there is more splash because the waves will not lift the bow. In a longer roll, though the waves may be higher, there is less danger of taking water. Sometimes, even with a lake model canoe, water will come over. In such cases it is well to move the load back, even to have the bow paddler sit back of his seat or thwart. This lightens the bow, which rises more easily and dryly with the wave. The question of ballast in all kinds of water is discussed in the chapter on precautions.

In paddling against a wind a regular stroke is almost impossible, if the waves are running high. Distance must be made between rollers and the speed eased up when a particularly vicious wave is met.

If waves are particularly choppy and, even with a lightened bow, insist on coming over, a clever bowman may escape a great deal of spray by jumping the canoe over each roller.

LAKE TRAVEL

An Indian taught me the trick. When the bow began to rise to the crest of a curler that threatened to come over, he would leap upward from his knees. Probably seventy-five per cent. of his weight would be removed from the canoe. The bow would spring upward and top the wave. As his weight descended the crest had been passed, and the bow would drop gently on the other side. It is a trick which should be attempted only by an experienced bowman.

While a good stern paddler may balance his craft perfectly as waves pass under him, he may add to the security by holding his paddle in the water. Many canoeists steady a canoe in this manner without realizing that they do so. A stern paddler also will unintentionally alternate his stroke with that of the bowman in bad water. This aids in maintaining a better equilibrium, as one paddle is in the water while the other is lifted for the next stroke.

The presence or absence of a load makes a big difference in the action of a canoe on a rough lake. A load increases the steadiness greatly. Too great a load results in a loggy craft that easily ships water. A light canoe with two men will dance buoyantly over the waves, but is extremely hard to handle. Its very buoyancy results in a lack of steadiness.

With a load allowing six or seven inches of freeboard in the center, perhaps the best results may be obtained with a sixteen-foot canoe. This affords protection from curlers, while the craft retains sufficient buoyancy to rise with a wave.

A canoeist who has been in the wilderness more than twenty years, has crossed practically every lake in Ontario, and that means thousands, and has had experience in the swift rivers of Quebec and Labrador, ballasts a light canoe with logs when there is a heavy gale or bad rapids to be run. The weight gives steadiness to the craft, the logs would come in handy if there were an accident, and the load will not shift or roll if several short limbs are left on the logs. A rock or two could be more easily obtained, but they might roll or shift their position and cause an upset, while, should there be an accident, they would be of no assistance.

The whole proposition of lake travel is one of experience and caution. A good canoe, properly loaded and handled, will perform wonders. A good canoeman and such a craft can live through anything short of a hurricane. But there is always a time when even the experienced man remains on shore. A slip of the paddle, the shifting of a pack, a moment of inattention, and disaster comes quickly and surely.

The best way to learn is to do it. Begin in light winds until the nicety and instinctiveness of balancing is perfected, becomes automatic. Then, within easy reach of shore, all sorts and conditions of wind and waves may be tried out until the canoeman learns what he can do and what he cannot do. Once he has discovered his own limitations and those of his craft, he is safe, provided he keeps within bounds.

CHAPTER VIII

RIVER WORK

FOR the skilled canoeman river work probably offers the greatest attraction. If it be a known river there is the joy of the swift, short dashes through white water. If it be an unknown stream there is the pleasure of the unexpected at every turn. New rapids must be studied and dared. Upstream there is the toil and risk of portage and pole. Downstream there is the fleetness and hazard of swift current and wrenching rips.

There are really five divisions in river work —the paddle, the setting pole, the tracking line, wading, and the portage. In the first three there is danger, and skill and experience are necessary for the successful journey. As with rough lake travel, definite instruction or rules can serve for little more than a guide.

The pole is used in upstream work, though many use one in running rapids. In swift water

RIVER WORK

and rapids there is no other way to make progress, under ordinary conditions. A five-mile-an-hour current nearly offsets work with the paddle. Passing up through rapids is impossible without a pole.

A pole should be ten or eleven feet long. One end should be shod with an iron spike, which can be attached by means of a cap fitting over the end of the pole and held on with nails. The spike may be carried in a pack and a pole cut and properly shod when it is needed.

Probably more skill is necessary in poling up through rapids than ever is required with the paddle. In eastern Canada, where there are many swift rivers, there are many men who travel up seemingly impossible rapids with comparative ease.

Perhaps the first thing a canoeist should learn is the power of moving water. He can do this in the little mill dam at home, where the inch-deep water from the sluggish creek, flowing through the apron, strikes his feet and shoots up over his head. The faucet in his bathroom will serve for the city man. A stream navigable by canoe may easily develop ten or fifteen thousand horse power. A man has only to thrust his paddle straight down in swift water and try to hold it there to learn how little is his own strength and how great that with which he must contend.

When the canoeman has duly appreciated the power of water in rapids he must not be misled by the seeming ease with which increasing ability with the pole permits him to ascend. The power is still there; he has only acquired the knack of evading it. He learns that success depends upon keeping the canoe headed straight into the current. To let a strong current grip either side of the bow more than the other means an advantage for the current with which his own puny strength is unable to cope. Once a canoe starts to turn, it instantly swings broadside and is swept back and down. If it strikes a rock there is instant disaster. If it plunges broadside into a heavy backlash there is little or no chance.

The skilled handler of a pole, by heading his canoe slightly one way or the other, can utilize the power of the current to carry him sideways without danger of being turned around. This is frequently necessary in changing from one channel to another or in avoiding boulders. It must be done delicately and carefully, however.

In such work the advantage of the canoe with ends higher than the bottom is seen.

There is less of bow or stern in the water, and less for the current to grip. The boat can be turned easily by the canoeman, but it is not turned so easily by the current as a straight-keeled craft.

When there are two men poling in the same canoe the work is easier and safer. Both can apply motive power, while the man in the bow may do much of the steering. This leaves the stern man free to expend more of his strength in shooting the canoe upstream.

Unlike paddling, both men pole on the same side. The application of power at the stern by pole is directly opposite to that by paddle, so far as the course is concerned, as it is a push, not a pull. In the bow the result is the same with pole or paddle. Hence, both poles must be used on the same side.

One skillful poler can do wonders in upstream work. Two can do the seemingly impossible.

To pole it is necessary, of course, to stand in the canoe. This is not so difficult as it seems, once the canoeman has acquired a natural or instinctive sense of balance. The pole helps greatly in keeping him steady.

The pole should be held with the left hand as near the top as the depth of water permits.

The right hand, held about two feet lower, should be stationary. The left hand slides out toward the end on the recovery, sliding down nearer the right when the greatest power is applied.

As the canoeman passes the point where the pole rests on the bottom he begins to apply the greatest pressure. He leans forward, and his weight and strength are both used in a quick propulsion of the canoe against the current. The knees bend, and he assumes a semi-squatting position when exerting the greatest pressure. The recovery and grasp of a new hold on the bottom should be accomplished as quickly as possible that the canoe may not lose all its headway or the bow swing so as to be caught by the current.

If one is not accustomed to poling, it is exceedingly tiresome work for a few days. After once being broken in, a man can pole ten hours a day or more with no greater exhaustion than from paddling.

In running rapids with a pole it is necessary to stand in a canoe, and here greater skill and experience are essential than in ascending swift currents. By beginning in less tumultuous rapids, however, the knack can be learned and the canoeman will discover that, as he can force the canoe against a current, he can also "snub" his craft quickly when going downstream.

In shallow, fast, boulder-filled water the pole is the better implement for running rapids. With the bowman using a paddle and doing much of the steering, the stern man, standing erect with his pole, is ready for instant action in stopping his craft or in swinging it across a current to avoid a boulder or gain a better channel.

Where rapids are deep and with only a few or no large boulders, use of the paddle in both bow and stern is the best method. Both paddlers should kneel, thereby increasing the stability of the canoe and affording greater safety in those strong, quick, lateral strokes necessary in changing the course of the craft. The bowman is of nearly equal importance with the stern paddler in guiding the canoe, and it must always be remembered that the canoe must move faster than the current if there is to be steerage-way. When the craft has been slowed down to the speed of the current, in changing the course from one channel to another or in avoiding boulders, it can be turned only by the paddlers reaching far out to the side and pulling it over by main strength.

Only experience gained by beginning with harmless rips and working up through more treacherous currents can tell the canoeman how to judge rapids and how to estimate his own ability to negotiate them successfully. He will learn the force of moving water and what his craft can do, will learn how quickly he can "snub" or turn, how to cross currents, and how to make use of currents in holding or changing his course.

Perhaps the best way to learn to run rapids is to climb them. Let the canoeman use a pole and spend day after day ascending some rapid-filled stream. A strong and necessary respect for the power of moving water will be instilled, and knowledge of the effect of twisting currents on a canoe will be learned with the danger greatly lessened.

Then, after a couple of weeks of the exhausting work, let the canoeman turn his craft and run down. He will pass three to six camping places in a day. There will be the exhilaration of rapid movement that seems more rapid after the long days of plodding. And he will know every rip, every twisting current, the location of every boulder. The slow upward journey permits careful inspection of each rapid and gives that knowledge necessary for successful downstream work. A trip of this nature will give a canoeman far more experience and skill than six weeks of running downstream.

With some canoeists success in running rapids breeds contempt. It is generally with such men that accidents happen. "I got careless just once and ran some rapids without studying them," is the way a mining engineer explained the loss of his equipment when making a run to James Bay. He and his companion lost everything except their canoe and lived on fish for six days.

One of the first things to be learned in river work is the ability to read the bottom of the stream by the surface. The depth of the stream, every boulder, each swirl and twist in the current, is seen instantly by the practiced eye. A trained canoeman will run a strange rapid after one glance downstream. Only a few of the essentials can be told here. The fine points of the game, the infinite variations, must be learned by experience.

A rock four inches below the surface will barely show, by ripples, in a four-mile current. In a twelve-mile current the same sized boulder will be easily known, though it is a foot or more below the surface. In swift rapids, where there is a great volume of water, rocks three or more feet beneath the surface throw up large waves. The canoeman learns to know when his canoe may strike such a rock and when it may pass over it in safety.

At first the canoeman will not be able to distinguish between waves and ripples produced by rocks beneath the surface and those caused by the swift current suddenly entering a deep pool beneath the rapids. Then the backlash, or waves, appear much like those caused by boulders, when in reality they are caused by the shock of swift water suddenly striking comparatively dead water, or by a volume of water so great that the channel does not permit a straight, even flow.

The backlash is not dangerous unless it assumes large proportions or the canoe drops into it broadside. Then it becomes deceptively so. Unlike rollers piled up by a gale on an open lake, waves in rapids are exceedingly stiff and uncompromising. They are high, curling, and close together. The canoe does not have the chance to rise and fall gently as on a lake, but, urged by the current, plunges directly into them before lifting. It is in such rollers, when they become three or more feet high, that a canoe will fill and sink so quickly

RIVER WORK

that the canoeman does not realize what has happened until he is in the water.

More accidents have occurred in rapids because of failure to estimate the backlash, or to handle the canoe properly in it, than from striking rocks. Once the canoeman is in the backlash, the only thing he can do is to hold his craft straight, ease the shock of striking waves as best he can, and keep an even keel.

Rocks in rapids are dangerous, but they are not so dangerous as popularly supposed. A canoe, properly handled, will never strike a large boulder in midstream if the boulder is so near the surface as to split the current. When a canoe does strike such a rock it is invariably due to ignorance of a simple rule in running rapids. A large rock near or above the surface in a large volume of swift water splits the current completely. Only the spray or a small percentage of the water passes over the rock. The strong, compelling water flows on either side.

In approaching such a rock it is only necessary that the canoe be kept straight with the current and a little to one side of where the split will occur. Then the current will take the canoe with it around the rock. The danger comes in making a quick turn to dodge the rock and permitting that half of the current which passes on the opposite side to grasp the stern. Then things happen so quickly that the canoeman probably never figures out just what did occur.

The canoe was turned to pass to the right of the rock. In turning, the stern was shoved into that part of the current passing to the left of the rock. There it was held and swept downward, the craft turning broadside to the current and being carried directly on to the rock. In such a position skill and strength are powerless, and the canoe is crushed or at least turned over and the canoemen and duffle spilled.

Many times, in running rapids, it is necessary to change from one channel to another. It is in this that great skill is necessary. Knowledge of the action of twisting currents is also essential that the water may be made to do as much of the work as possible. It is necessary first, of course, that the canoe be moving faster than the water that there may be steerage-way. The stern paddler must do most of the work, for the bowman, by pulling the bow to one side or the other, offers the current an opportunity to grasp the canoe broadside. The stern paddler should pull the stern toward the direction in which he wishes to go. The current will swing the bow, although the bowman should hasten the movement. In this way the canoe may be lifted sideways, or slightly diagonally, until the new channel is attained. Sometimes, in swift but comparatively open water, it is possible to shoot diagonally down and across, but the canoe must be traveling much faster than the current.

The beginner should never offer the bow of a canoe to a vicious bit of fast water, nor should he ever attempt to travel straight across a current. In ascending rapids it is a good rule always to keep the bow headed straight into the current until the canoeman has learned to use the current in changing the course. A member of the Canadian geological survey lost his life because he attempted to go straight across a bad stretch of rapids. The current and backlash flipped the canoe over instantly.

There are times when tracking, or lining, a canoe is easier and safer than poling, while the trouble of portaging is unnecessary. Many rapids can be ascended in no other way, the volume or speed of the water making poling impossible.

The line should be run through a ring in the bow of the canoe and fastened to one or two thwarts. If the canoe is heavily loaded and the current very swift, much of the strain may be eased and distributed by passing the line beneath the packs in the bottom of the canoe and fastening to a thwart in the rear. Then any sudden strain is expended on the line beneath the packs and not on any one point in the canoe. When there is no ring in the bow the line should be given a turn on the shore side of the bow thwart and fastened to a rear thwart.

One man can pull a heavy canoe up a bad stretch of rapids. His companion should walk along the shore opposite the craft and keep it off the rocks. If there is much tracking to be done, a tump line used as a breast or shoulder strap will make the work much easier for the man ahead.

Sometimes rapids are so shallow it is necessary to wade and pull the canoe. The work is made much easier if there is a man at either end to lead the craft across currents and around rocks and shallow places. One man alone at the bow often has a difficult and exasperating time of it.

In summing up the question of negotiating rapids, it might be said that it is the most dangerous phase of canoeing, that it never is completely safe, that the utmost skill, caution, and watchfulness must be exercised constantly, and that no other form of canoeing offers so much sport to the man who has mastered his craft and himself.

CHAPTER IX

PRECAUTIONS: BALLASTING THE CANOE

THE seasoned wilderness traveler learns many precautions, recognizes signs of danger, and realizes the value of compromise and stealth as opposed to that of blind, bulldog fighting, while the novice continues unconcernedly, miraculously avoiding dangers which he does not see or recognize. The novice learns slowly, unless disaster has brought him up with a start, or a series of narrow escapes has taught more quickly the necessity of eternal caution when on a canoe journey.

Drifting down a stream in the midst of civilization or traveling through the wilderness, there is always the possibility of danger around the next bend, beyond the next point. Rapids, falls, treacherous currents, gathering storms, sudden squalls, hidden rocks—each of the many possible dangers of the wilderness is taken as part of the day's

PRECAUTIONS

work by the woodsman and guarded against or anticipated accordingly. The man traveling through a country for the first time, especially if he is not a skilled woodsman, must be on his guard continually. His map may not tell him of every rapids or falls and his ignorance of local weather conditions does not permit his forecasting storms or estimating their possibilites.

The woodsman, if he knows his country, many times travels by weather. That is, he forecasts the weather in the morning and picks his route accordingly. If he sees signs of a heavy wind or quick, strong squalls, he will choose the lee shore of a large lake, even though he must paddle more miles to reach his destination. He may even forsake a straight course down big lakes and make a detour through sheltered streams and small lakes. If he does not know the country he will study his map well at night or before starting in the morning, estimating his chances of crossing big stretches of water, noting islands and points that will afford shelter from a strong wind and permit him to "sneak" around an open stretch.

The seasoned traveler in a land of large lakes does most of his traveling before nine o'clock in the morning. Under ordinary conditions, the wind seldom attains much strength before that time. To be up at three o'clock and in the canoe by four means half a day's travel before a storm makes further progress impossible. The woodsman will study his route and so time his journey that he may strike big, open stretches of water in the early morning. If he knows his country well, he will do most of his traveling after sunset, sleeping in the daytime.

There are days on large lakes when travel is impossible at any time, and there is no alternative except a tiresome wait on shore. The sunset lull may offer a chance of escape, although, in stormy weather, this may last only ten or fifteen minutes, hardly enough to risk a dash across a three or four-mile stretch in which the dead swells are still rolling.

Weather conditions vary in different parts of the country, and forecasting at best is a gamble, but there are generally several signs of squally weather which are common anywhere. A close, hot day generally means a storm in the night or the next forenoon. In some parts of the country certain winds prevailing for a day bring a storm. The canoeist should learn these weather indications in the country in which he is to travel and avoid open stretches when there is a possibility of a quick, sharp squall or strong wind.

While this is important, it is also essential that the canoeist know what he can do and what is impossible for him and his craft under certain conditions. He may cross a stretch of open water in a strong, steady wind in perfect safety, but he should always estimate the nature of the wind and of the waves, look for possible shelter in an emergency and know exactly how much his canoe will stand and how much he himself can contend with.

In traveling in a new country care is necessary in descending rivers. Ordinarily falls or rapids make themselves heard in plenty of time to permit the canoeist to get to shore. But sometimes, when a strong wind is blowing, or the river is making sharp turns in rocky gorges, one will turn a bend to find himself at the brink of a falls or rapids.

People who live in such a country and know the rivers thoroughly will sometimes run the top of a bad stretch of rapids and thereby shorten their portage as much as possible. Care should be taken in such places not to overrun the portage. Upstream, of course, there is practically no danger.

The question of ballasting a canoe properly comes best in such a chapter, for upon the distribution of the load in a craft depends safety as well as ease in travel and dry duffle. No matter what the distribution fore and aft, the weight of the load should always be placed as low as possible. If there is room to lay a pack flat on the bottom, it should not be stood up. If there is not room on the bottom for all the packs, those containing the heaviest articles should be placed beneath those containing tents and blankets. A low load not only means greater stability and safety, but offers less surface to the wind.

In ordinary travel, in open water or in rivers, the bow should ride two or three inches higher than the stern. Many canoeists put an unnecessary drag on their craft by placing the bulk of the load in the stern.

In running down a swift stream or traveling before the wind, a canoe should be on a nearly even keel.

In bucking straight into a heavy wind the bow should be greatly lightened. If two men are traveling with a very light load or with no load at all, it is better for the bowman to move back nearer the middle. A light bow means a drier canoe.

PRECAUTIONS

In running before a gale the canoe will handle better, and will be drier, if the bow is as far down as the stern.

In traveling upstream, especially when poling, it is better to have the bow ride much higher than the stern. The canoe handles more easily, as there is less opportunity for the current to grip and twist the bow, and greater progress is possible.

The advisability of having a light bow and stern in a heavy sea or in rapids with a bad backlash is seen when a man paddles his canoe alone from the center. Bow and stern rise and fall easily with each wave, and the lone canoeman, while he may not make the speed, gets through with a dry craft and with practically no danger of upsetting.

To travel on the principle that there is to be no opportunity for an upset is the best way to keep dry duffle. If, however, the canoeist wishes to take chances on windy lakes or in rapids, he should at least take the precaution of lashing the more important pieces of his equipment to the canoe. This may be done, if packsacks are used, by simply unbuckling a strap, passing it over a thwart, and rebuckling it. If duffle bags are used, a tump line may be attached to a thwart, run through the handles at the ends of the bags and attached to another thwart.

The canoeist should never venture into the wilderness or far from a base of supplies without a repair outfit. Manufacturers invariably will furnish directions for repairing their craft and will supply the necessary materials. As a rule, it is better to obtain such an outfit at the time the canoe is purchased. If this has not been done, a can of Ambroid or a good canoe cement, some copper tacks, and several small squares of canvas will do. White lead is furnished now in friction top tins and is excellent for repairs.

In case of a tear in a canvas canoe, the torn edges should be pulled back, white lead, canoe cement, or Ambroid placed on the planking and the canvas stretched back and tacked down. An outside coat of white lead or cement completes the job. With a wooden canoe it is generally necessary to shape a thin piece of cedar between the ribs and the batten strips on the inside, tacking it on with copper tacks after first coating it with white lead or Ambroid.

A yoke furnishes the best method of carrying a canoe weighing eighty pounds or more, especially if trails be rough.

CHAPTER X

THE PORTAGE; METHODS OF CARRYING CANOES; THEIR CARE

THERE are many methods of carrying a canoe, each generally depending upon the size and weight of the craft, the custom of a particular district, and the prejudice or hobby of the carrier. A twelve-foot birch, weighing only twenty pounds or less, may be taken across a portage by simply thrusting the arm beneath the middle thwart and carrying it as a woman would a market basket.

With such a canoe, or one weighing as high as fifty pounds, the canoeman may, if there is nothing else to carry, throw it onto his shoulder, one side resting on the shoulder and the other against his head. In both cases the paddles are placed inside.

With light canoes, however, it is very easy and simple to carry a packsack as well, and then the canoe must be turned over and carried bottom side up. This may be done in any one of three or four ways. The canoe may be turned over on the pack and the middle thwart rested on the back of the neck or on the pack itself. Few canoes are made, however, with a thwart exactly in the center. Generally the middle thwart is placed four to twelve inches aft.

There remain the two accepted forms of carrying—with the paddles or with a yoke. Some Indians employ a fourth method and carry the canoe by a headstrap or tump line attached to a stiff pole lashed to the middle thwart and on top of the gunwales.

With a canoe weighing less than seventy-five or eighty pounds the paddles probably afford the best method. There is no extra contrivance to be adjusted or to get lost, just one less piece in the equipment. To carry a canoe with paddles, thongs or strings should be tacked to the center and rear thwarts. They should be so arranged that the paddles can be easily slipped in and out and yet be held securely. The paddle blades should be placed on the center thwart and the other ends at the stern. The blades should be far enough apart to permit them to rest on the shoulders without cramping the neck muscles.

THE PORTAGE

While a canoe may be carried on paddles with the center thwart some distance from the exact center of balance, the canoeist will be wise to have his canoe built with the center thwart exactly in the center. Then, with the paddles properly adjusted, the weight is distributed between the shoulders, by the paddle blades, and the back of the neck by the thwart. The spring of the paddles is eliminated, and the canoe will carry much more easily.

With either method, if there is not enough natural covering for the bones, a shirt or sweater thrown across the shoulders will serve. Patented air pillows and pads are only something extra to be cared for and accomplish no more than a good woolen shirt.

The Indian seldom attaches his paddles to the thwarts. Generally he places the shafts on the center thwart and the blades on the bottom of the canoe. He will hold them there with his hands as he swings the canoe over his head. But he has a light canoe and has been doing that sort of thing for several hundred years. The white man will have less trouble if he has his paddles lashed.

Several forms of yokes are manufactured, and, where one man is to carry a canoe weighing eighty pounds or more, they will be found an advantage over the paddles. A stiff paddle will hold such a canoe, but it is not the best implement for its principal use.

The original, home-made yoke, and one now being manufactured, consists of two parallel bars reaching from gunwale to gunwale and braced about eighteen inches apart. Sometimes wooden buttons hold the yoke to the gunwales, or it may be made to fit a certain canoe tightly. But generally it is loose, the weight of the canoe holding it in place. The loose yoke is a great disadvantage, however, in getting the canoe to the shoulders and back to the ground.

With such a yoke the shoulder contrivance is made in one of several ways. Generally two broad strips of canvas are tacked to the two crossbars, running parallel to the canoe and resting on the shoulders. Sometimes these strips are made of rawhide or other leather, and canoemen have been known to tack a large piece of raw moosehide to the two bars and cut a hole through which to thrust the head.

One of the first manufactured yokes was patterned after the old-fashioned, hand-carved water bucket yoke. This will serve very well if there is a proper method of attaching it solidly

THE PORTAGE

to the canoe. At first the canoeman fears it will twist his head off if he should stumble, but a little experience shows that one can easily extricate himself.

The best yoke for carrying a canoe is that generally sold in the United States. It consists of a single crossbar which has a curve of several inches in the center to make room for the neck. On each side of the center is a wooden block covered with a leather, hair-stuffed pad. When the canoe is in position, these pads rest on the shoulders and make carrying as comfortable as is possible.

One caution must be exercised in purchasing such a yoke. See that the two pads are attached to the crossbar by thumb screws and are adjustable. One make of yoke has fixed pads, whereas men do not have the same width of neck or of shoulders. A yoke with the pads too close together is impossible.

A little experience will show that a canoe is carried more easily when the carrying contrivance is so fixed that the stern is heavier than the bow. One hand grasping a gunwale then balances the canoe perfectly, while there is no obstruction of the view of the trail.

When a canoe becomes too heavy for one man, or if no one in the party cares to portage an 125-pound craft alone, two men may carry the canoe. Experienced canoemen are unanimous, however, in the opinion that one man may carry a canoe more comfortably alone than with the aid of another, even when the weight exceeds one hundred pounds. Further, there is one less trip across the portage and back.

When two men carry a canoe it should be carried bottom side up and lifted above their heads. The man at the stern then lowers his end until the gunwales rest on his shoulders. His companion lowers his end until the front thwart rests upon the back of his neck and shoulders. Both men then have a good view of the trail, while each may carry a light pack. It should be remembered, however, that the man in front has more than his share of the canoe. Further, if he finds that the thwart is painful, he can lash the paddles to the center and forward thwarts.

Due to ignorance or carelessness, the canoe receives more abuse on portages than anywhere else. Manufacturers have built a remarkable craft for its pounds, but it will not stand everything. The canoe is built for a purpose, a purpose which it alone can fill, and, for the very reason that it will carry heavy

THE PORTAGE

loads and still can be easily carried itself, it must have its weak points.

These weak points need never be put to the test if the canoe is properly built and is properly handled. Remember that a craft weighing sixty-five pounds can carry nearly half a ton, but that the sixty-five pounds are spread out over a length of sixteen feet and a width of three. Naturally the supposition should be that no great weight should ever rest on one point or small surface. See that the weight is always distributed, don't try to prove a manufacturer's claim as to what his product will do in a freak test, and your canoe will live much longer and continue to give good service.

Following these simple rules without exception means fair treatment for your canoe:

Never load a canoe which is not floating freely.

Never run the bow or stern of a canoe onto the shore; always come up to the land broadside. Step out into the water rather than to rest the craft against a rock, snag, or gravel bottom.

Never take a canoe from the water unless it is empty and can be easily handled.

Never load a canoe on shore and then drag it into the water.

Never lift the bow of a loaded canoe onto a rock or onto the shore. Unload it, or tie it and let it drift.

Always be careful in stepping into a canoe to let the weight down gently, and after making sure that there are no rocks or snags beneath the craft upon which your additional weight will force the bottom.

Never sit on or in a canoe on shore.

To seasoned canoeists some of these rules may appear useless, if not actually an insult. But there is not one of them that is not broken hundreds of times a day, while the men who observe them all are rare.

But caring for the canoe properly and obtaining the most adaptable method of carrying it does not end the subject of portaging. In some districts the portage is an ever-present problem. A portage may be marked on a map, and it may not. Even if marked, it may be on either side. There are a few north country portages which are on islands, rapids, or falls forbidding passage by canoe and the nature of the shore prohibiting an easy carry. Portages leading from lakes to other lakes, or to rivers, may start most anywhere. In fact, a stranger in the wilderness more often than not spends much time looking for the trail over which he must carry his burden. Frequently the take-off is not blazed. It may start from a flat rock on which there is no trace of a trail, or its end may be hidden behind rocks or bushes in a cove.

The experienced woodsman does not have so much trouble, for he has learned how to look for a portage. He knows that a portage, no matter where, how or why, was made by men who sought the shortest and easiest way between two lakes or around a falls. In fact, he looks for the obvious place for the portage rather than for the blaze or the beginning of a trail.

Traveling on a river, he knows, naturally, that there will be portages around bad rapids and falls. When he encounters such a place he looks first at the hills on either side of the stream. He looks down the valley to see if the river bends. If it turns to the left, he looks to the left bank for the beginning of the portage. If it be high water, he looks close to the top of the falls or beginning of the rips. If the water is low, he looks farther up. If there is a short stretch of rapids that can be easily run, and quiet water between it and the more vicious rips beyond, he will run through and look for the portage where the quiet water ends.

On a lake the woodsman will watch the

country back from the shore rather than the shore itself. If he knows where the lake or river into which he must portage lies, he will study the intervening country, look for a bay running back in the right direction and then pick the lowest point in the hills behind the shore.

None of these rules is hard and fast, but in the main they are to be relied upon. The exception occurs only where unusual geological formations make unusual portages necessary. There are times, too, when thick brush or windfalls caused the original portage makers to take a longer route because it could be more easily cut out.

In the north country there is invariably one distinguishing feature at each end of every portage—the tea stick. The Indians and the woodsmen boil the pot often in their travels, and, should there be no blaze or trail to mark the take-off of a portage, the traveler should look for the blackened sapling thrust into the ground or propped across a rock.

CHAPTER XI

PACKING; VARIOUS METHODS; THEIR ADAPTABILITY

PACKING, which here means the receptacles for various articles taken on a journey and the method of carrying the same, is one of the most widely discussed problems of the canoeman. Each district has its general method, and each individual has his variations and adaptations of that method, or a combination of several.

The original and perhaps most common method of packing in North America is with the head strap, or tump line. Some enthusiastic delvers have discovered that this is of Asiatic origin. It is so simple and adaptable, however, that it can be understood how its origin may have been spontaneous wherever people found it necessary to transport burdens.

Because the method, used by the Indian and adopted by the French voyageur and

Hudson's Bay Company packer, is the most universal, experts in wilderness travel have given it not only first place but declare there is no other adequate method. Their declarations are always predicated on the fact that it is the method universally used by the Hudson's Bay Company packers.

However, there are few canoeists whose journeys are similar to those of the fur packers. The fur brigade takes out many bundles of pelts, each package weighing about eighty pounds. In the large canoes used there may be twenty or more such packages. It would be out of the question to have a packing contrivance attached to each. So the canoeman attaches his tump line to a bale or two of fur, carries it across, unties the tump, and returns for another load.

If a canoeing party is to take a long trip into the wilderness, and carry supplies for many weeks, the tump line is an excellent contrivance for packing. But where the journey is to be for only two or three weeks, the problems of the exploring expedition or the fur brigade are absent, and it does not necessarily follow that the tump line is still the best or only means of portaging.

There is one fundamental thing in the matter of packing that should be first understood. Any method means hard work and is productive of much torture for the beginner. Muscles become hardened and accustomed to the strain in time, but packing is always hard work. Whatever ease may be attained is mental rather than physical. The stronger the muscles become, the bigger the load a man will carry that the number of trips may be lessened. He can look upon a portage with equanimity only after he has reached that state of mind where he can see the carry as an inevitable part of the day's work, something that can be made easier only as the time devoted to it is lessened.

Tump line or pack harness, pack basket or pack sack, each will torture at first, each affords hard work. And for the short trip canoeist, the subject resolves itself more into a question of convenience and adaptability than anything else. To determine this it is better first to describe the various methods.

The tump line may be used especially well with the small, waterproof duffle bags commonly taken into the wilderness. The tump line, which consists of a broad piece of leather with two long thongs of leather fastened at each end by sewing or buckles, may be attached to one or more duffle bags. These are then lifted to the back and the broad band placed across the top of the forehead, most of it above the hair line. The thongs should not be so long that the load comes below the hips, nor so short it rests high on the back. With this load adjusted the packer can toss additional duffle bags on top, letting them rest against the taut thongs, his shoulders, and the back of his head.

With a pack cloth the two thongs of the tump line are stretched along either side about a foot from the edges and the edges turned over them. The duffle is piled in a compact heap in the center of the cloth. Sharp or hard articles should not touch the cloth. The sides are folded over the duffle and the thongs pulled tightly, as are puckering strings, and tied around the bundle. A blanket may be used in place of a pack cloth.

The pack harness generally consists of shoulder straps and a head strap with thongs attached for tying the contrivance to any sort or size of bundle. One style of pack harness has a long bag attached with extra folds of duck to hold additional duffle.

The pack basket is a receptacle woven from oak splits or other wood and having two shoulder straps attached. Sometimes it is covered with waterproofed duck. Unlike most packing contrivances, its capacity is unalterable. Neither is its rigid shape adaptable for canoes.

The packsack, a Minnesota product, is becoming more widely known and used each year. Until a few years ago it was unknown except in Minnesota and western Ontario. Like the pack harness in the eastern States, the pack basket in the eastern mountains, and the tump line in Canada, it is a distinctively local contrivance, but one which, for the short canoe trip, offers the best solution of the packing problem.

The packsack is a large bag of heavy duck with two shoulder straps and a head strap attached. A large flap covers the top of the bag and is strapped down. The bag is carried by the shoulder straps and the head strap across the forehead. Its size and its construction permit any load up to its maximum capacity, and no adjustment of straps is necessary with small or large load.

Packsacks are made by several firms in Minnesota and Ontario, and there are as many degrees of efficiency. The ideal packsack should be made of heavy, waterproofed duck with leather shoulder and head straps. The head strap should be attached far down on the side of the bag and the shoulder straps far enough up so that the load does not hang away from the back. Sizes vary from a small bag for a light load to the blanket sack, which will carry half a dozen blankets.

Still another packing contrivance used by many canoeists is the lunch box of wood, fiber, or light sheet iron. In this, dishes and the lunch food are packed, the box being carried by a tump line or placed on the top of a pack. These add ten to twenty pounds to the weight and are awkward and inconvenient in the canoe or on a portage.

In packing with a tump line the limit of the load is the packer's strength and experience. With the pack harness it is difficult to handle much more than seventy-five pounds, although other packs may be placed on top, once the pack is in place. With the pack basket there is a rigid limit to what may be carried. The packsack's limit in food is about 125 pounds.

When packsacks are used one or two lighter packs may be carried on top of the first pack. There is no doubt but that the adaptability of the tump line makes it possible to carry the heaviest loads with such a contrivance, provided the packer was born with a tump line

One or more packsacks may be thrown on top of the first pack.

across his forehead. But the canoeist seldom attempts more than 125 to 150 pounds, and such a burden may be carried with the packsack as well as with the tump line, better, if the packer be new to the game.

The packing question then resolves itself into what is the most convenient for any particular trip, provided the packer is new to any of the above contrivances. A man who has always used a packsack will have great difficulty in using a tump line.

"It's not what's the best rig, it's what a man's used to," is the way a guide summed up the question.

In a canoe trip in the wilderness of two or three weeks the complete outfit, including food, for two men may be carried in two large packsacks. With the exception of a rifle or rod case, everything, including the axe, will go into the two sacks.

On such a trip four of the small duffle bags and a pack cloth are necessary to transport the same equipment. The same is true of the pack harness or the tump line used only with pack cloths or blankets.

If many portages are to be made, the question of loading and unloading is exceedingly simple with packsacks. At the portage the two packs are lifted from the canoe, and the canoe is empty. If one man takes a forty-pound pack and the canoe, the other can take a 125-pound pack. Each lifts his burden to his shoulders and starts. The paddles and rod cases are in the canoe. The man with the heavy pack takes the rifle. Except for a possible sour dough pail, there are no loose objects to be tied to packs or carried in the hands. There is no tying or untying. At the end of the portage the canoe is placed in the water, the two packs dropped in, and the canoeists are off.

With the tump line there is the inevitable tying of the packing contrivance and the adjustment of loads at one end of the portage and the untying and loading of six packs instead of two at the other end. To be sure, the duffle bags to which the tump line is attached may be placed in the canoe without untying the straps. But, if all the duffle bags are tied, it is difficult, sometimes impossible, to ballast the canoe properly with so large and cumbersome a bundle.

More time is lost on canoe journeys in loading and unloading at portages than in any other way. Where many portages are to be made in a day, hours may be wasted in gath-

PACKING 115

ering the equipment together at each portage. With packsacks there is nothing to do but lift out the pack and place it on the back.

Further, a canoe may be carried with a light packsack. When two men are making a journey this means only one trip across a portage. If the portage is a mile long, each man walks a mile instead of one or both making a return trip and walking three miles. With a tump line it is not possible to carry a canoe and a pack.

Packing duffle in the bags is another important feature of the subject. The large, openmouthed packsack is easily packed, and it is large enough to take anything in camp. There are no small bundles or articles to clutter up the canoe or burden the hands on the portage. The grub sack is set up beside the fire, and, if it is properly packed, dishes and food for the noonday meal are on top and ready at hand. The bag does not have to be unpacked and then packed again.

When a long journey, where supplies are to be carried for two or three months, is to be made, the subject of packing differs. Tents, blankets, and personal duffle carried in packsacks may be easily and quickly taken out each night and repacked in the morning. A week's supply of food and the dishes go in another packsack. But the surplus of food is carried better in the small, waterproofed duffle bags, which may be carried with a tump line or on top of the packsacks. The packsack, with its large mouth, cannot be made water-tight, though it will shed rain all day in the canoe or on the trail. But the duffle bag excludes dampness, thereby preserving the food and preventing an increase in weight.

As the length of the trip, the number of men, or women, in the party, the presence or absence of guides, varies, the adaptability of the various contrivances differs. If you are going into a new country and will use a guide, learn what method he employs. If he is a packsack man, and you have provided only tump lines, your troubles will begin at the first portage. If you are new to the packing game you will find the packsack most readily adaptable. With both shoulder and head straps, you can distribute the load and carry more comfortably. With any outfit, remember that it is going to hurt, and that all you can do is to stand it until muscles and philosophy have become adjusted.

CHAPTER XII

BEDS AND BEDDING

AS each form of out-of-door activity has its special equipment, the canoe has one all its own. The man who travels into the wilderness by pack train, flat boat, auto, wagon, or launch has only the capacity of his vehicle or craft to consider. The man who travels by canoe must consider the capacity of his own back as well as that of his craft, while the number of portages and average daily run necessary to cover a given route in a given time are deciding factors in a large part of the equipment.

The man who travels alone on foot, or with only a saddle horse, must consider weight and space more than any other traveler in the wilderness. Next comes the canoeman, for, while he may carry half a ton easily in the canoe, he cannot carry his canoe and that same half a ton over portages and make progress or get any particular pleasure out of his trip.

The man who takes a trip down the Ohio, Mississippi, Missouri, Tennessee, or any of the innumerable smaller rivers in the United States or in northern Wisconsin, for instance, where lake after lake may be traversed without a portage can stock up with all the pet paraphernalia that long winter evenings have evolved. If he should strike a power dam, an express wagon will take everything around for a dollar or two.

But the man who goes into the north country, either in northern Minnesota, Maine, or any of that infinite stretch of canoe land in Canada, whether it be for two weeks or two months, must consider carefully everything he takes. It is a subject upon which volumes and countless articles have been written, although for the enthusiastic voyageur the subject never grows old. It is called " going light but right," a phrase so elastic that really it is worthless as a descriptive title. One man may go " light " and, so far as he is concerned, " right." But another would find himself deprived of things he considers necessities if he had the same outfit. One man is perfectly willing to make two or three trips on each portage to transport that which he considers essential to his happiness, while another gladly goes without things that he and his companions may " clean up " in one trip across each carry.

"Light but right," despite the manner in which it has been dinned into the ears of the outdoor man, cannot be a matter of hard and fast rule but of individual choice, taste, and degree of experience. In fact, so variable is this much sought perfection in equipment that it seldom remains the same, even with the individual. The first time out a man overburdens himself, and the second year he flies to the other extreme. The third time he is more rational and becomes a crank on equipment. He weighs and measures and changes things each year until he has an efficient outfit. Then he begins to want more comforts, and the weight increases. If he meets a man with the identical equipment he himself had five years before, he jeers at it.

Since hard and fast rules cannot hold against individual beliefs and wishes, the subject can be approached properly only from the bottom. The fundamental principles, the deciding factors, only can be stated authoritatively. The individual will build upon them to suit himself. He alone can decide what is essential to his comfort and to just what extent he is willing to burden himself that he may have it. Some men seem to take actual pleasure in depriving themselves, though in reality their pleasure comes afterward, when they relate how little they carried.

These things are essential to anyone on a canoe trip: Food, cooking utensils, shelter, bedding, and clothing.

These things are essential if daily journeys are to be made: Food that will quickly rebuild tissues exhausted by long hours at the paddle and yet which may be cooked quickly and easily; cooking utensils which are light, compact, durable, efficient, and of sufficient variety to permit changes in menu; a shelter which is light, just large enough to protect men and equipment, and can be easily and quickly erected; bedding that is warm but light and requires little or no care; clothing that protects from cold, sun, flies, and rain, all in one, so that a complete change is not necessary.

You can build up a carload on that, or you can fill one packsack and yet meet every requirement. You are the one to be suited, the one to carry the equipment. You have only yourself to please, only yourself to blame.

Manufacturers and individuals have devised infinite pieces of equipment to meet the needs enumerated above. In this and succeeding

BEDS AND BEDDING

chapters the questions of bedding, tents, clothing, etc., will be considered. Those articles which have been proven most efficient will be described. Any opinions stated are based upon a somewhat varied experience and upon observation of equipment of nearly every type of wilderness traveler, from the millionaire with an expensive outfit to the timber cruiser or prospector who has spent his life in tents and canoes.

The nature of the bed must depend largely upon the nature of the trip. Where there are no portages, a light mattress or inflatable air mattress may be carried, while as many quilts and blankets may be taken as there is room for. Only remember that a cotton quilt will absorb moisture, is hard to dry, and becomes very cold and clammy.

But on a trip where there are many portages the bed must be light, although some canoeists insist on taking a sleeping bag. These contrivances weigh from sixteen to thirty pounds and have other objections. Some combine blankets, or quilts, a waterproofed covering, and an air mattress. A man may burden himself with these things and believe he is justified in so doing, but experienced woodsmen never use a sleeping bag, or, at least, the contrivances usually placed on the market. The objections are these: They are too heavy for the comfort obtained, the waterproofed covering keeps all the moisture from the body within the bag, and the blankets become cold and damp or must be dried every day, and there is no benefit in using a waterproofed bag when sleeping in a tent. To sleep without a tent in mosquito season is torture.

The experienced woodsman uses a single blanket or a sleeping bag without a waterproofed covering. Such sleeping bags, made of llama wool or camel's hair, afford the maximum warmth for the minimum weight. A sheet of tanalite or good waterproofed cotton should be placed under such a bag to prevent dampness from reaching the sleeper from below.

A mining engineer who has been in every part of Canada has chosen such a contrivance after many years of experimenting. The entire outfit weighs only three and one-half pounds. It is sufficiently warm for the summer and early fall. Moisture from the body escapes readily, leaving the bag dry. In winter this man places an eiderdown quilt inside the camel's hair bag. It brings the total weight to ten and one-half pounds and is warm enough for most anything south of the Arctic Circle.

This is the ideal sleeping equipment. The mattress, of course, is of balsam or spruce boughs, which, in addition to their romantic feature, offer the cheapest, easiest, quickest bed, once a man has learned to make one properly. The one objection to the above sleeping bag is the cost. The total for the complete winter outfit is about fifty dollars. The summer equipment costs nearly twenty-five dollars. But it is the only feasible sleeping bag. Only the novice will take the heavy, unsanitary clammy affair generally offered for sale.

The man who cannot, or will not, make a bough bed has the best substitute in an air mattress. These weigh from nine pounds up. Be sure to buy one that is quilted. One big air sack is a difficult thing to sleep on. If the sleeper moves he slides or rolls off. This mattress can be placed most anywhere and is inflated by the lungs.

The common form of bedding is the lone blanket. The man who cannot afford camel's hair or llama wool turns to the pure sheep's wool affair, which, while it is much heavier, furnishes all the comfort necessary if there is skill in making the bed. The best camping blanket is the Hudson's Bay Company's famous affair. The four-point weighs twelve pounds and is seven and one-half feet long by six feet wide, doubled. The three and three and one-half-point blankets are smaller, but of the same thickness. The three and one-half, weighing ten pounds, is the most adaptable size. Such a blanket should be purchased in the white or khaki colors. The wool is unscoured and retains the natural animal grease, thereby being almost waterproof. There is an imitation of this blanket. The genuine bears the company's seal always.

The out-of-door sleeper soon learns that as much cold comes from beneath as from above and the sides. A rubber blanket keeps out most of this, but a sheet of tanalite or a waterproofed tent floor better answers the purpose. For the same reason the bough bed should be well made and thick.

The novice often has difficulty in making such a bed, although many books have described methods. The boughs are easily gathered by cutting down a balsam and dragging it to the camp site. There the limbs are quickly cut off with an axe. The larger branches are placed on the ground first, with

BEDS AND BEDDING 125

the bow side up. This furnishes the spring. Then they are thatched with smaller branches, the process beginning at the head and being carried to the foot, the soft tops covering the butts. There is no necessity of making too long a bed. Enough to keep the hips and shoulders off the ground is sufficient.

If it is necessary to carry balsam some distance to the camp site it is most easily done by "limbing" the tree where it is felled and carrying by the woodsman's method. The axe head is placed on the ground and the branches hooked around the perpendicular handle. A man can carry enough for a good bed in one load.

In a country where there are no balsam or pine, willow tops, first year's growth, will be the best substitute.

A good bed is one of the most important things in camp life, and the canoeist should study his methods until he attains perfection. A cold bed, or an uneven one, will not afford the rest a hard day demands. Even the pillow should not be shirked, though your companion may say he is satisfied with his shoes. A cotton bag weighs nothing, and it may be stuffed each night with an extra shirt, socks, or sweater.

CHAPTER XIII

TENTS FOR CANOEING

THE canoe tent must be: light, easily and quickly erected, have enough floor space for sleeping and for storing the outfit, and be fly-proof. A large number of models and mosquito contrivances have been devised. None of them is perfect, for the reason that any such tent is a series of compromises. The best can only have the maximum of advantages with the minimum of drawbacks.

On a canoe journey the tent is taken down each morning and set up each night. At the end of a long day's paddle, when camp is to be made and a meal cooked, the simplest tent becomes the best. The tent is used only for sleeping and protecting the duffle from the weather. Therefore it need not be large nor with much head room. For cold or rainy days in the north country it should be possible to throw open the front and build a fire in

This canoe is loaded for a two week's trip, two persons. Note the absence of small articles and the ease with which the craft may be loaded or unloaded when packsacks are used.

This tent requires two poles and seven stakes. The cheese cloth door is tucked in under the floor. There are no poles or guy ropes to be in the way. The best qualities of the ideal canoeing tent are combined in this shelter.

the doorway. Camp may be made at the end of a rainy day; there should be a bottom or floor of waterproof material.

To meet these requirements the following tents have been devised: The old, standard "A," or wedge tent without a wall; the miner's, or pyramid, tent; the Frazer tent, an adaptation of the miner's; the baker, or shed, tent, with a rear wall, straight sides, slanting roof, and front awning which serves as a door; the lean-to, which is best for fall when the flies have gone; the canoe tent, with either peak or short ridge, which is a combination of the "A," miner's, and baker; the Hudson Bay tent, a combination of the miner's and "A" styles; and, lastly, an adaptation of the miner's tent which brings the peak forward and affords a straight wall in front.

Nearly all of these tents may be set up by using ridge ropes instead of poles and attaching them to trees. Such a method is generally unsatisfactory because of the time wasted in finding trees in the right places and in grubbing out between them. In mosquito season camp should be pitched in the open. A tent never fits well with a rope ridge, and a badly fitting tent does not shed water or wind adequately.

If poles are used with any of these tents according to the old style, they are in the center of the floor space or of the door in all types except the baker and lean-to. By using an outside ridge pole attached to the ridge by tapes, the center and door poles may be eliminated, but at the cost of cutting double the number of poles. With the baker, canoe, and "straight-front" miner's tent, guy ropes are necessary. These require time and are irritating obstructions.

After trying and studying every type and method of erecting, the writer settled upon the following as, in his opinion, the most efficient and most quickly erected tent for canoeing purposes: A miner's tent was ordered without the hole in the peak for the center pole. Instead, a strong canvas loop was sewed into the solid peak. The flaps at the front were made eighteen inches wider, so that they lap more than three feet when tied. On a rainy day they may be staked out, a fire built in front, and cooking done from the shelter of the flaps. A floor of waterproof duck was sewn to the bottom of the tent on the sides and back. The dimensions are seven feet three inches square by seven feet three inches high at the peak. The material is light, waterproof cotton, and the total weight is fourteen pounds. With a tanalite floor the weight would be eight or nine pounds and the tent even more serviceable.

The method in erecting the tent is as follows: The bed is built on the ground. Two poles ten feet long are cut with crotched ends. Seven stakes are required. The tent is stretched over the bed and staked down. The crotched poles are inserted in the canvas loop at the peak, and the tent is up.

Attached to the canvas loop at all times is a piece of cheesecloth large enough to cover the entire front of the tent. In mosquito season this is spread across the door immediately when the tent is erected, the bottom being folded in under the floor.

Such a tent has the following features: Its steep sides shed water perfectly, and its pyramid shape offers no opportunity for the wind to grasp it. The floor insures a dry tent, no matter how damp the ground. The bed is beneath the floor, and there is always a clean, dry place on which to spread the blankets. The floor and the cheesecloth keep out all flies, mosquitoes, midges, snakes, insects, and small, camp-prowling animals. There is room for three persons and their equipment. Two persons can stand erect at the same time. The wide flaps enlarge the tent on a rainy day or may be staked out perpendicularly on cold nights and permit a large fire in the door.

The tent has one drawback. On a rainy night the door, which slants back to the peak, must be tied. This is of minor importance when the advantages are considered. The Frazer tent eliminates this by having an awning over a narrow door. But this requires guy ropes or poles, and the small door does not permit a thorough drying or warming of the tent by means of a big fire in front. By increasing the size to nine by nine feet, such a miner's tent would easily accommodate four men and their equipment.

When there are four men in a party, however, the question of speed and ease in erecting the shelter is of less importance than where there are two. It is then that a good baker tent becomes adequate. More poles are required, but there are more men and axes to cut them. Such a tent is exceptionally good for wet or cold weather, while in mosquito season cheesecloth stretched across the front, and with a taped slit in the center, keeps out the flies. For a comparatively small weight in shelter, many men can sleep in a baker tent.

TENTS FOR CANOEING

The other styles find their adherents for various reasons—more head room, more floor space, accustomed use, etc.

The day of the canvas tent for canoeing is long past. Several varieties of light-weight, waterproofed cotton are on the market. A khaki or green color is better than the white, being less attractive to flies and softening the glare of the sun. Tanalite has the advantage of not leaking even if it should fall down. This feature permits the storing of duffle against the walls. The material selected should not only shed water but should not absorb moisture. Then its weight is not increased if packed on a rainy morning.

A floor sewed to the edges of the tent gives the best protection from dampness, draughts, and insects and is the most efficient and easily handled form of floor cloth. Many canoeists use a separate piece of waterproof duck, which is spread out in the tent on top of the sod cloth, or inside flap sewed to the edges of the tent. This is not absolutely insect proof and forms a separate article. The last is an advantage, however, when the floor cloth is used for packing with a tump line.

Mosquito netting or bobbinet are not adequate insect excluders in the north country, though farther south they are sufficient. Cheesecloth is, and it permits a free circulation of air. Some use a secondary tent of cheesecloth suspended inside the tent. This only adds to the trouble of getting in shape for the night and is not so efficient as the cheesecloth door tucked under the tent floor. Still another system is a door of cheesecloth sewed in all around, entrance being through an opening in the center closed with a puckering string. The disadvantage in this lies in the fact that the tent cannot be thrown open to a fire in cold or rainy weather.

In deciding on your tent, don't aim for any single advantage. Weigh everything, consider every possible contingency, the values and defects of every device. Don't seek the perfect tent, for it does not exist. The nearly perfect tent is the most efficient compromise.

CHAPTER XIV

COOKING UTENSILS, COOKING, AND FOODS

MODERN equipment has made it possible for the canoeist, with a minimum of weight and bulk in his culinary outfit, to obtain the maximum results, always provided, of course, that he knows how to handle it.

For a party of two, the following list comprises every article necessary for the preparation of as good a meal as may be desired: Three kettles, one frying pan, one mixing pan, one folding baker, three plates, three cups, a mixing spoon, and two knives, forks, and table spoons. Nothing else is necessary for the proper preparation and service of a meal.

An aluminum alloy has been used to make the best type of cooking utensil. Stamped from one piece of non-corroding, tough, long-lived metal, the aluminum kettles are as near perfection as possible. The only objection to them, that advanced by users of packsacks, is that the shape is not adaptable to their method of packing. The same model of cooking utensils is made of pressed steel. It is only slightly heavier than the aluminum and costs less than half as much.

These kettles are round and are made to nest and fit in duffle bags. An oval nesting kettle is in universal use among cruisers in northern Minnesota. The three or four pails are light and easily packed in a packsack. They are not, however, stamped from one piece.

Aluminum frying pans were discarded immediately, and those of steel substituted. To permit nesting with the aluminum kettles and dishes, these pans have been made with several varieties of detachable or folding handles. All are intended for use with a stick. With such an outfit all the kettles, pans, frying pan, plates, cups, knives, forks, and spoons may be nested compactly and carried in one canvas bag. With the oval cruising pails for the Middle West the frying pan is made with a two-inch handle to which a square loop of steel is attached to permit the insertion of a wooden handle.

It must be remembered in choosing any

COOKING UTENSILS

cooking or packing utensil that tin rusts, that fruit strong in acids should never be kept in tin kettles or push-top tins and, preferably, even not cooked in them. Sour dough, if kept in a tin receptacle, causes much rust. A graniteware or aluminum pail is best.

Aluminum cups, because of the rapid manner in which the metal conducts heat, are impossible. Many do not like aluminum plates for the same reason. Weight may be saved by having the mixing pan of aluminum. So-called "white metal" forks, or those of aluminum, are best. Aluminum spoons are strong and light, while the old steel case knife is sufficient.

Bakers are made of tin and aluminum. The aluminum bends out of shape easily, but is a little lighter. The baker whose sides form a peak at the rear is of too obtuse an angle to do good work and will not brown bread or cake on top. There should be a perpendicular wall of two or three inches behind. The tin baker is little heavier and more easily set up and taken down. With either, the reflecting surface should be kept bright. One with a nine by twelve inch pan is large enough for three or four persons.

With these utensils to choose from, the

canoeist may obtain a light, durable, efficient outfit. If the cost is a factor, he may buy the cheaper equipment of tin, pick up an aluminum mixing pan and spoons and graniteware, tin or aluminum plates at a department store sale and purchase a twenty-five-cent frying pan and have the hardware man cut off the handle and attach a square loop for a stick. All should be packed in one or two canvas bags to keep the black kettles and pans from other duffle in the pack.

All food should be carried in muslin or light duck bags. These can be purchased, ready waterproofed, as cheaply as they can be made. The waterproofing does not insure dry food, but it keeps out dirt and does not absorb moisture. There should be an assortment of small push-top tins for pepper, matches, spices, soda, and baking powder, and larger ones for tea, coffee, and bacon grease.

Add an axe to the tent, blankets and cooking utensils, and the canoeist's equipment is complete, with the exception of his personal outfit, treated in the next chapter. The axe, in summer, need be only a half or quarter axe with twenty or twenty-four-inch handle. Never take the toy hatchet offered for sale. A leather sheath permits placing the axe in a pack. If the axe is packed in the food pack each morning, it is out of the way except when needed and will not be lost. In fall a full axe should be carried, as the large amount of wood required makes the hand axe inadequate. A necessary accessory is a file for sharpening the axe and a whetstone or oil stone for sharpening both axe and knives.

The question of camping food is limitless. The canoeist making an easy journey in a civilized country need have no anxiety, as he can transport nearly everything he wishes. The man going far from a base of supplies must look carefully over his food list, and he will check it off and study it for several years before he arrives at his ideal supply.

The party taking a trip of two or three weeks may carry several things in the line of luxuries, especially if each member be an able packer. When a trip of one or two months is to be made, and supplies for the entire trip are to be carried, only the essentials are possible.

The woodsman, born and brought up in the wilderness, requires much more food than the man who goes to the forest only for recreation. The woodsman eats more than is necessary, but he is a peculiar individual and wants all that he eats. He won't work without it. The city man, accustomed to light breakfast and luncheon and sedentary habits, is suddenly confronted with violent physical exercise and a greatly increased appetite when he goes into the woods. He thinks he eats a great deal, but he does not, in comparison with the woodsman.

A prospector who has spent a lifetime in Ontario and other parts of Canada has a list which he has proven many times. He counts on the following for men who work for him: One pound of flour, one pound of bacon, one-third pound of dried fruit, and one-third pound of beans per man per day. Rice, sugar, tea, salt, salt pork for beans, butter, and canned milk bring the total per man per day to more than three and one-half pounds. He does not like to bother with butter, but is compelled to take it to keep the men in good humor.

Such a ration would last a city man two days and probably three. The reason for citing it here is to give the city man an idea of how he must prepare for the appetite of a guide.

Many books and articles have been written on the subject of food, and tables have been formed. But individual taste and preference

COOKING UTENSILS

is so great a factor that lists are of little value except to furnish ideas and for checking. Let the canoeist remember these facts and then build up his list of supplies accordingly:

Four, beans, rice, sugar, and fats are necessary to produce muscle and energy.

Dried fruits are necessary to tone the system and offer variety in a plain fare.

A preponderance of fats is injurious in warm weather.

The great drain on energy results in a craving for much sugar.

Cornmeal should be eaten sparingly in summer. It is an excellent fall or winter food.

Butter, though a good food, is a habit, and its absence will be forgotten in a few days. To carry it is a nuisance.

It is well to carry one luxury. For some this is evaporated milk, for others jam or conserves. Let the individual decide what it shall be and then carry it.

The question of cooking food is so closely linked with the question of food that they should be considered simultaneously. A good cook can prepare appetizing, nourishing, adequate meals from the dozen or so essential raw materials. If there is such a cook in a party, both weight and bulk may be greatly reduced. Kephart condensed the entire subject of out-of-door food and cooking into one sentence—" The less a man carries in his pack, the more he must carry in his head." *

The good cook will know the following and also know how to meet each problem:

The three principal kinds of foods are carbohydrates, fats, and proteins. The first two produce heat and energy, the last forms gas, water, and waste material.

Proteins remain in the stomach twice as long as carbohydrates, and fats even longer.

Proteins and fats are, as a rule, easily and quickly cooked. Carbohydrates are not available as foods until broken down by thorough cooking.

This sounds uninteresting and scientific, but it is the essential foundation of efficient cooking and eating in the wilderness. Proteins, which remain in the stomach longer, should be served at the morning and noon meals, to prevent an empty stomach and an "all-in" feeling before the next meal. Carbohydrates produce the necessary energy and heat, but they do not "stay with you." Further, they

---

*Camp Cookery, Outing Hand Book No. 2.

COOKING UTENSILS

require much cooking. Therefore, the wise cook will:

Serve pancakes and bacon for breakfast they will remain long in the stomach, and also a well cooked cereal, because it is a strength giver.

Serve well cooked beans, baked or boiled, at noon. They have a large percentage of carbohydrates and in addition are nearly one-fourth protein. Biscuits, baked at breakfast, or sour dough bread, and sauce, complete a well balanced noon-day meal.

Serve rice with sugar and cream at night. This is a valuable food and easily digested. It leaves the stomach quickly, and the man unaccustomed to heavy eating as well as heavy exercise gives his stomach as well as his muscles a rest when he goes to bed. Rice served alone at noon is not enough. It furnishes sufficient food value, but it is digested so quickly a man cannot work well until the next meal.

The above is intended as a skeleton idea. Around the framework of slowly digesting but nourishing meals morning and noon and nourishing but easily digested meals at night, the good cook may build an infinite variation. He must also remember that apricots are essential the first few days, as well as a few raw onions, to keep the suddenly overtaxed system in order. He will know that raisins are exceptional as they do not have to be cooked to make them available as a food. So quick is their action they really are a non-injurious stimulant.

A little forethought in planning and preparing is a great aid in obtaining quick and adequate meals. The cook should study his map closely. If he has a day with no portages before him, he may spend the preceding evening in the preparation of several things that can be easily carried in the canoe, but which would be a nuisance on a portage.

Sour dough may be carried in a pail or push-top tin. By mixing in additional flour each night, the breakfast pancakes are easily provided for, and the harmful baking powder is eliminated. Sour dough bread may be raised over night and baked at breakfast time.

Cookies may be baked in the baker after supper, or during the preparation of the evening meal, and carried in a large push-top tin. If there are no portages the next day, a pie made the night previous will reach the noon lunch unharmed. Sour dough bread or bak-

COOKING UTENSILS 143

ing powder biscuits should always be baked in the morning for the noon-day meal.

Beans, if baked in a bean hole over night, or boiled after supper until soft, can be carried in a push-top tin. They insure an efficient meal the next noon. If there are no portages in the afternoon, sauce may be boiled at noon for the evening meal.

CHAPTER XV

CLOTHING

MEN from cities who have gone into the wilderness because their business took them there, and kept them there year after year—mining engineers, railroad engineers, explorers, and geological survey members—invariably admit that the native knows best how to dress and to live in his particular section, and that the outsider has less trouble if he adopts local methods.

Such men go into the wilderness to work, and not for recreation. Their work consumes most of their time, and they demand, and get, efficiency in equipment. Once they have proven the worth of a thing, they stick to it, unless their work takes them into an entirely different sort of country.

The recreationist, because of less experience and greater enthusiasm, is prone to go to extremes in the matter of tents, sleeping equipment and personal duffle. Until years of experience have brought wisdom, he is inclined to burden himself, or others, with useless paraphernalia, or articles which are carried for a month and used only once or twice.

Outfitters have developed some wonderful bits of equipment, and, when the cost is a lesser object, the canoeist planning a trip in any district cannot do better than to seek the advice and obtain the goods of an efficient firm. He should be cautious, however, to seek a really good outfitter and to get the advice of an experienced man rather than that of a clerk who never has demonstrated the value of anything he sells. When they can be afforded, aluminum kettles and pans, imported woolens for clothing, the best in footwear, and light, compact medicine chests, toilet kits, and shaving outfits are valuable not only for their lightness and compactness but for their durability and all-around efficiency.

The man who has less money to spend can enjoy himself just as thoroughly and travel just as efficiently if he studies the methods of the people who live in the land he will visit and gets most of his equipment there. Such a method should be founded, however, upon personal experience and observation or upon first hand advice.

The matter of dress and personal equipment is one of the most important the canoeist has to consider, and one open to nearly as many interpretations as there are canoeists. Between personal whim and outfitters' ideas, the touring canoeman presents a strange medley in attire, from the sleeveless rowing shirt of the college boy to the elaborate patented articles of his father. Their wide divergence in methods of dress is particularly noticeable when contrasted with that of the woodsman, which is universally the same.

On the Mississippi, Ohio, and eastern rivers where days and nights are warm, portages are absent, and the capacity of the canoe alone limits the equipment, personal wishes can dictate the clothing to be worn and carried without uncomfortable results. A trip through the north country demands protection from flies, cold days and nights, rain and thick brush. Experts are unanimous in declaring that only wool should be worn. The woodsman wears only wool, unless he is living in a permanent camp during hot weather, when he dons a cotton shirt and overalls or khaki trousers.

But if a given route is to be covered in a given time, and each day spent in the canoe, rain or shine, the woodsman wears woolen underwear, a woolen shirt, woolen trousers, and heavy woolen socks. Many men who live and work in the north country wear the same heavy weight of underwear the year round.

Some men will not wear wool next to the skin and depend upon waterproofed garments for protection. One can learn to wear wool comfortably, however, and the slight discomfort of the first few days will be more than compensated for later.

With woolen clothes, mosquitoes cannot bite except on the hands, face, and neck. A man can portage, or paddle, all day in the rain and, even though he finally may be wet through, will still be warm as long as he has wool next to the skin and keeps at work. When he has finished the day's toil, he can build a fire and dry out. The man who does not change from wet to dry clothes rarely catches cold when he wears wool.

Woolen clothing, if of a good quality, will shed rain for many hours. When portaging on a brushy trail, the moisture will beat through, but under such conditions nothing except rubber is a protection. Heavy socks are desirable because they keep the feet from being chilled when wet. Even the best of shoes will not always keep the feet dry.

The greatest objection to waterproofed cotton garments is that they are seldom, if ever, waterproof, and that, when once wet, they are cold, clammy, heavy, and difficult to dry. Light weight oil slickers, or coats which reach nearly to the knees, give excellent protection from the rain, but they cannot be worn on a portage or the wearer will be as wet from perspiration as he would have been from the rain. Even when paddling, they will be found uncomfortably warm, unless the day be very cold. If the canoeist is willing to carry the extra pound or two, and the extra article, he will find an oilskin coat valuable in camp on a rainy day, but hardly anywhere else.

The river driver of Michigan, Wisconsin, and Minnesota has spent more than fifty years living under conditions more adverse to comfort than the canoeist ever encounters, and his clothes are always of wool. He starts to work when the ice goes out, and is out in the rain, snow, sleet, and wind, sometimes up to his waist in water, from daylight until after dark. His feet are always wet. Yet his outfit consists, almost without variation, of the following: A heavy suit of underwear, heavy woolen trousers cut off below the knees, heavy woolen socks, heavy woolen shirt, and driving

CLOTHING

shoes. Even though wet through, he keeps warm when working, and at night there is a big campfire beside which he dries out. When tired out, he goes to sleep in his wet clothes.

The canoeist journeying in the north country cannot do better than to adopt a similar costume. The ideal equipment in a country where frosts come in early August and it may snow in the first two weeks of June is as follows:

One suit of light woolen underwear to be worn every day.

One suit of medium or heavy woolen underwear to be used for sleeping, a change when the other suit is being washed, or for exceptionally cold weather.

One pair of light woolen trousers. These should be of hard finish so as not to catch brush and should be woven sufficiently well and closely to prevent tearing on snags. Kersey and light mackinaw are the best.

One light woolen shirt, gray or tan. One is enough. It can be washed on a bright day and dried en route, the wearer paddling in his undershirt alone.

Three pairs of heavy woolen socks. This gives a dry pair for sleeping and a dry pair each morning.

One heavy stag shirt. This is a lumberjack's garment and one that only in the last year or two has been recognized by a few out-of-door enthusiasts as a valuable piece of personal equipment. The lumberjack and river driver "stags" his trousers by cutting them off with a jackknife below the knees. He found a coat too heavy and cumbersome to work in, so he bought a heavy shirt and "stagged" it by cutting it off around the middle of the hips. Later manufacturers learned this and placed the stag shirt on the market.

The lumberjack has been wearing it for years. It is made of heavy wool, generally about thirty-six ounces to the yard. The pattern is the same as that of a "top" shirt, except that there are no skirts, or tails. It affords nearly as much warmth and protection as a coat and yet fits so snugly, and is so light that it may be worn without interfering with the free use of the arms and body. This shirt is now being manufactured for sportsmen with several pockets sewn around the bottom. Some are made with a puckering string, giving the shirt the appearance of a boy's blouse. The plain, unpocketed shirt is best, as it will not catch on snags or brush.

With such an equipment the canoeist is pre-

CLOTHING

pared for any sort of weather down to zero. In fact, the lumberjack wears such an outfit all winter. It may prove warm on a portage through a breezeless swamp, but the portager would perspire as freely if he wore nothing except light cotton, and he is saved a chill when he leaves the hot swamp for a windswept lake.

With this equipment the only extra pieces of clothing to be carried are the heavy underwear, two pair of socks, and the stag shirt. Many carry a sweater, but the stag shirt serves every purpose of such a garment and has the additional advantages of shedding rain and being windproof. The stag shirt is an excellent pad beneath the canoe yoke or paddles.

It is taken for granted that every article of clothing described will be of pure wool. The wearer should carry a bar of naphtha soap for laundering. With it he can wash wool in cold water.

In the fall a pair of heavy woolen gloves should be worn.

The question of footwear has so many angles that it is difficult to give definite rules. Many canoeists wear the so-called hunting boots and carry canoe moccasins. This means an extra article to carry and care for and loss of time in the changes at each end of a portage. If one can stand the single piece of leather for a sole, the best footwear for canoeing is the shoepack of Maine and Canada. Well made, it is waterproof, easy as a moccasin on the foot, and, with the usual canoeist, adaptable for both canoe and portage. Some men cannot, however, wear a shoe without a sole on rough ground. A shoepack is made with an extra sole, which affords better protection from rocks and roots, but is more liable to leak.

In purchasing a shoepack the canoeist should see that the sewing is sunk below the surface of the leather. Otherwise, the thread will be cut. On a trip of more than a month, he should be provided with waxed thread for repairs and a small can of dubbin, or grease, for softening the leather and keeping it waterproof.

Many woodsmen wear a shoe, usually hobnailed, exclusively. This may prove hard on the canoe, especially if any natural awkwardness forces a heavy descent every time the wearer embarks. However, if the canoeist can stand the single sole and does not intend to travel through rough and rocky country, he will find the shoepack the best article of footwear possible.

CLOTHING

The low moccasin, without protection around the ankle, is only a useless bit of equipment, serving no purpose that compensates for its cost or transportation.

As a guide or example of the possibilities of cheap but adequate canoeing equipment, and not as a model, the following description of the author's outfit for two persons is given:

Two large packsacks, one for food and dishes, the other for tent, blankets, and personal duffle. If the trip is to be for more than two weeks, a third and smaller packsack is taken.

A miner's tent as described in a previous chapter.

One four-point Hudson's Bay blanket weighing twelve pounds and one lighter wool blanket weighing five pounds.

One towel, one cake of soap, comb, brush, and shaving outfit for each person, and small medicine chest, camera, water-tight box for films, and small package of needles and thread.

Extra suit of woolen underwear for sleeping and change, two extra pairs of woolen socks, one stag shirt of heavy wool per person.

Three nesting oval kettles of tin, tin folding baker, tin cups, aluminum spoons, "white metal" forks, steel case knives, and large aluminum mixing spoon. The pails and cups nest and are packed in a canvas bag. The spoons, knives, and forks are carried in a pocketed roll of canvas. This is spread and tacked to a tree, with wooden pegs, beside the campfire each night.

An aluminum mixing pan, a twenty-five-cent frying pan with the handle cut off and a steel loop attached, and graniteware plates are packed in a second canvas bag.

All food is carried in waterproofed cotton bags. Several small push-top tins carry tea, coffee, bacon grease, pepper, soda, baking powder, and matches. A large push-top tin is used to carry cookies, sauce, beans, or pea soup prepared the night before. A small graniteware pail, carried in the hand, holds sour dough.

An axe, a file, canoe cement, a trolling line wedged in the bow of the canoe—that is all. With a sixty-five-pound canoe, complete equipment and food for two weeks, the total weight, canoe and all, is only 210 pounds. The outfit has seen hard service for three years, some of it having been in constant use for eighteen months.

CHAPTER XVI

MAKING CAMP: ADVANTAGES OF SYSTEM

IF a canoeing party be wise, much time will be spent in the first few days studying and devising a system and plan of co-operation in making and breaking camp, in preparing the noon-day lunch, and in portaging. Whether the trip be one of idle drifting, each morning bringing the first plan for the day's journey; whether the route be down a river in the midst of civilization, a systematic division of labor, a just assignment of duties, and enforcement of their proper performance are essential for the greatest progress or enjoyment.

System means more leisure if the trip be of the non-objective, Indian variety; more time for fishing, for excursions back from the water, for photographing, and for simply doing nothing. On a hard journey, where every available minute is spent in putting distance behind, system not only tends to comfort and ease but is an essential factor in speed.

Whether there be two, three, four, or eight in a party, there is no reason why supper should not be ready three-quarters of an hour after the canoes touch shore. In the morning, with the same number, camp should be broken an hour after the campfire is started. The preparation of the noon-day meal should not take more than fifteen or twenty minutes, leaving a half-hour for rest before the resumption of the journey. Speed in loading and unloading at portages, in each quickly starting with his pack or canoe, means many miles added to the day's total.

System gives the same advantage to the party making the leisurely journey. If camp is to be broken in the morning, the more time there will be for exploring, taking pictures of beautiful spots, or any of the other activities various members of the party may desire. If camp is to be maintained in one place for several days, a quick breakfast and dishwashing mean more leisure for everyone.

No party starting on a canoe journey will achieve perfection in its sytsem for several days. The members must master unaccustomed tasks, wear the rust and clumsiness from their bodies, revive little knacks in doing things, and ascertain to which individual certain tasks should be assigned because of particular proficiency. Once this has been definitely settled, things will move orderly and smoothly, it being taken for granted, of course, that there are no shirks.

Much time may be saved and trouble avoided by a systematic packing of whatever contrivance is used for carrying food. If the journey be short, and there is only one small bag for each article of food, those which are seldom used should be placed at the bottom. Especially in packing in the morning should care be taken and the packsack or duffle bag so arranged that everything necessary for the midday meal is at the top and may be taken out without a search through the entire bag to find the wanted article in the bottom.

As the canoeist may learn much from watching the woodsman, he may also greatly increase his knowledge, and add to his comfort and safety, if he watches the Indians. The red man always camps in a good spot and rarely, if ever, sets up his tepee near large timber. He always picks an exposed point in early summer and a thicket in the fall. The white man can do no better than follow the Indian's example.

Tall timber is dangerous, especially in midsummer, when the strongest winds prevail. A cleared point, with exposure to the breeze on all sides, is the best camping spot when flies are thick. Islands frequently afford ideal spots of this nature, but camping on islands is hardly advisable. A drifting canoe, a spell of bad weather, and heavy winds, may hold the canoeist a prisoner, with possibly disastrous results.

The forest traveler should study the weather and not seek the exposed point when a heavy wind or rain storm is threatening. Then the shelter of small poplar or birch, even with the mosquitoes present, is preferable.

Later in the year, when the flies have thinned and the evenings are cool, spruce or poplar thickets afford the best camping spots. These are generally found back of sand beaches, and it is seldom necessary that brush must be cleared or roots and stumps grubbed out.

When camping near a sand beach the tent should be set well back from the sand, however. To camp on the sand, or even to stop

MAKING CAMP

a beach for lunch, generally results in sand tting into the clothing, blankets, packs, and food bags.

Prevailing winds should be studied and guarded against. In many districts south and west winds generally bring rain in summer, and quick squalls invariably come from these directions. An east wind sometimes brings a steady rain. For this reason it is advisable to face a tent toward the north or northeast, that storms coming up in the night will not blow down a tent before it can be closed.

Never leave a tent with the flaps untied. Any good tent will live through a gale if properly erected and tightly closed. Permitting the wind to enter may easily result in the shelter being torn to shreds or blown down and damaged beyond repair.

When canoeing in the fall a dense thicket generally offers protection from any direction. Care should be taken, however, that no pine or poplar stubs are near the tent.

One of the advantages of the systematic operation of the camp will be the proper care of everything each night. If the tent is not large enough for the duffle, the food bags should be placed on a raised spot or logs and covered with a tarpaulin or placed under the canoe. If the canoe is not used for this purpose, it should be carried up from the water each night, turned over and weighted down with stones or a heavy piece of driftwood. A sudden storm in the night cannot blow it into the water or break it by blowing it against rocks or trees.

No matter what the weather, it is an excellent rule to take good care of the canoes each night. If rabbits are numerous, the canoes should be left right side up and the paddles placed inside. Rabbits will gnaw varnished wood or that salted by perspiration. In any case, paddles should always be laid inside the canoes. Left on the beach or on rocks, they may be stepped on and broken. If not broken, they will be scratched and marred by rocks and become a source of irritation to the hands.

If a trip is to be made on the Ohio or Mississippi rivers, canoes should always be carried far enough from the bank to prevent their being touched by the wash from big river steamboats. Some small rivers rise and fall quickly from natural causes, and others may do the same because of the opening or closing of a dam. Special care as to the stowing of canoes and selection of camp sites should be exercised on such streams. They

MAKING CAMP

are indicated by fresh high-water marks, driftwood, and mud flats.

In the late summer many streams are so low they are difficult to navigate, even by canoe. In choosing a route by map, beware of those rivers shown in a thin, crooked line.

In the late summer or early fall, when the days are shorter and there is pressing need for many hours of travel daily, it is often possible to make a late camp by counting on the possibility of sleeping without shelter. If the canoeist be a good judge of weather, he can foretell a clear night, and a bow bed, with the tent drawn over the sleepers to keep off the dew or frost, is all the preparation necessary. In doing this it is better to eat supper at five or six o'clock and then travel as long as daylight lasts. The paddlers will find themselves as comfortable beneath the stars as they would have been inside a tent.

To the novice all these things come slowly, unless he be so fortunate as to have companions of great experience, possesses keen observation, or has that natural aptitude for the out of doors with which some men are gifted. Those who seek the pleasures afforded by the canoe and the infinite waterways of this continent without guide or experience have a great reward in the exercise of ingenuity, the overcoming of obstacles, in developing a creative instinct. Those who have had experience, no matter how much, will always learn something new, can always anticipate the unusual. For the canoe, though the oldest craft in America, has inexhaustible possibilities for those who know it and have come to respect it.

THE END

CPSIA information can be obtained
at www.ICGtesting.com
Printed in the USA
BVHW04s2324120818
524318BV00009B/36/P